MY JOURNEY THROUGH RACISM

No BLACKS, No IRISH, No DOGS
BEING BRIGHT BUT NOT CLEVER

Pearson Nurse

authorHOUSE®

AuthorHouse™ UK Ltd.
500 Avebury Boulevard
Central Milton Keynes, MK9 2BE
www.authorhouse.co.uk
Phone: 08001974150

First published by AuthorHouse   03/25/2011

ISBN: 978-1-4567-7536-0 (sc)
ISBN: 978-1-4567-7535-3 (e)

This book is printed on acid-free paper.

Contents

Author's Note

Racism is the belief that the genetic factors which constitute race are a primary determinant of human traits and that racial differences produce inherent superiority of a particular race. (*Wikipedia free Encyclopaedia*)

Police harassment and brutality directed at black men, women and children date back to the days of slavery. Such police action across the nation today reveal important aspects of commonplace discriminatory practices of individual whites and white dominated institutions that allow and encourage such practices. (*Wikipedia.org*)

This book is a compendium of my personal experiences and perceptions throughout my life and gives factual examples of covert and overt methods of racism practiced by both individuals and institutions and was encouraged by a young black student who was subjected to racist behaviour and was looking for a way to overcome those feelings of dejection. He felt that some black people could well benefit from the experience I've had and thus prepare themselves accordingly.

ACKNOWLEDGEMENTS

This book has been shaped by the feedback of my family and friends who have been instrumental in advising and mentoring me through the progression of my journey through life thus far.

I dedicate this book to my parents who have since died and were the main inspiration to my success. May God bless and keep them in all eternity.

I also give special thanks to my wife Lorna who supported and encouraged me in this venture.

Important insights were added by my friends :- Duncan (Tom) Riley, Ronald Skeete, Dudley Rhynd, Alvin and Shirley Sandiford and some members of family who also contributed to the production of this book. To them, I am most grateful.

PROLOGUE

For much of the past, the reality for too many black people has been one of disaffection, disappointment and despair. More often than not, our dreams of empowerment are sent back with a rejection stamp from the main stream stating; 'NO YOU CAN'T'. Those words have echoed through so many generations that many of us have accepted them as the truth because of the laws that are socially constructed and imposed by the dominant group within a geo-political boundary and used to restrict the progress of black people.
(Essence Magazine)

Example: The introduction of draconian repressive measures by the racist regime of South Africa which empowered the police to shoot down black people which included a number of school children during one of the many demonstrations against apartheid. *(discrimination on the grounds of race)*

The larger lesson for us as a people is that we can mend our broken dreams and redefine what is possible.
"YES WE CAN" .*(Barack Obama)*

We have the power to solve our own problems and achieve our own dreams. All we have to do is to realise our potential and manifest it. What we want is already ours, we need only to believe it to make it real.

The doctrine of black inferiority was the ideology on which racism was founded and was constructed by European exploitation, brutality and bestiality against African slaves and later against colonies.

CHAPTER 1

Introduction

I am a retired College Lecturer, a cricket fan, a lover of soul, reggae, classical and S.O.C.A. music, a sports and fitness enthusiast who enjoys the company of his wife, family and close friends.

I am a native of Barbados and have lived in London for more than twice the time I've lived in Barbados. I do not consider myself a Londoner and have a deep sense of love for my family, my friends, my beautiful island in the sun and its people and humanity in general. Identity is very important to me.

Barbadians are a proud people; this pride is based on our perception of ourselves: that we are educated, intelligent, resilient and sociable.
Our cultural strengths are based on what we have inherited from our African ancestors and the Europeans during slavery and colonialism:

We have very little natural resources but there is an abundance of human capital which we must invest for the benefit of the nation and future generations.

I had a very humble upbringing in a culturally rich part of Barbados known as "Carrington village", a small bright, black but poor community, made up primarily of chattel houses, grocery shops, rum shops, churches and pharmacies, nestled between Bridgetown the Capital to the west, Government house (*the residence of the Governor General*) to the east and Belleville, (*an affluent white community that is comprised of beautiful colonial houses, lush royal palms and lovely gardens*) to the south.

The village was renowned for its vibrancy and meaningful political discussions in the evenings under the street light in this part of the village named as Quakers Road where most of the adults would gather to informally discuss generally; what is going on in the Island.

These informal debates provided a wealth of information to us as youngsters. They also enlightened and educated us 'in more ways than one' and generally kept us informed in matters relating to life in general. We looked upon these adults as the 'second House of Assembly of Barbados', 'the shadow cabinet' as some might say.

Many famous national figures emerged from the belly of this very significant part of the Island.

I have several brothers and sisters, all of whom contributed to the welfare of the community and are still to an extent, continuing this work with the less well able members of our beloved community. My family were also hugely successful in their educational endeavours.

As a young boy, I tended to keep special friends, some of whom were very special to me since we shared common interests, indulge in the same kind of mischief and were very proud of our heritage and educational achievements. It was important to us that we achieved our potential and set examples to the younger children following in our footsteps. As we grew older, we took it upon ourselves to help to educate the younger children in the community and encouraged them to be the best they can. My siblings, my friends and I were fortunate to achieve meaningful positions in society mainly because of our attention and dedication to our education and family values.

Director, Professor in Political Science, Architect; Surveyor; Lecturer; Inspector of Taxes; Manager; Company Director; Lawyer, etc. are proudly mentioned on our c.v's

(It is widely known that 'A man is known by the company he keeps')

I spent my formative years at Combermere School, fondly referred to as the 'Watford University' due to its location at Watford in the parish of Saint Michael. It is the oldest Secondary School in Barbados and also one of the oldest in the entire Commonwealth. With its motto 'up and on', it was the first to offer secondary education to the lower class blacks on the Island and is considered to be one of the top Secondary Educational Institutions in Barbados. I consider it an honour and a privilege to have been part of this educational establishment.

Sanctuary Buildings Great Smith Street Westminster London SW1P 3BT
tel: 0870 0012345 dfes.ministers@dfes.gsi.gov.uk
Rt Hon Charles Clarke MP

30 October 2004

Dear Mr Nurse

I did not want to let the occasion of your retirement pass without thanking you for
the contribution that you have made to education throughout your career. Teaching
is such an important job that makes a real difference to the lives of individuals and
to the well-being of our society. Thank you for all you have done.

With best wishes for a long and happy retirement.

Yours sincerely

Charles Clarke

department for
education and skills
creating opportunity, releasing potential, achieving excellence

INVESTOR IN PEOPLE

CHAPTER 2

Barbados as a fun loving and caring society.

Barbados is a culturally rich island with a population of approximately 300,000 people. Our 'Island in The Sun' serves as a popular destination for foreign holiday makers and as a paradise for the super rich as well as the local inhabitants because of its fine beaches, friendly caring people, the laid back approach to life, the entertainment, the safe environment, Oistins fish market on Friday nights, the beautiful scenery, the all year round warm weather and the numerous other attractions that make it one of the most pleasurable places on earth and to quote Sir Cliff Richards, "My little bit of paradise".

|*A view of Oistens Beach from the roadside. (All of the beaches in Barbados are public)*

Growing up in Barbados was fun and a dream that most Barbadians have for their children who were born in the UK. There is a wealth of activity for adolescents 365 days a year:-

Another one of the popular beaches in Barbados

Children playing on the beach in Barbados

Cricket, football, basketball, hockey, athletics, table tennis, swimming, creative activities, etc. to name but just a few.

There was no television during my youth in Barbados but despite this, we were spoilt for choice and therefore had very little time to become bored. There were times when football was played barefooted on rough surfaces with a tennis ball. The loss of toe nails and other injuries caused by the rough surfaces was an everyday occurrence but that never stopped us from enjoying ourselves.

A miniature form of cricket was also played where the players knelt one knee to bat and to bowl. The bat, ball, stumps and pitch were all approximately half of the regulation size and the rules were changed in order to create more fun. Beach cricket was played on the sand at the edge of the tide as it rolled back into the sea. This area, used as a wicket, provided the most solid part of the beach while it was still soaked with water and generally caused the ball to generate more speed as it bounced off the sand. A tennis ball and a makeshift bat sometimes made from a coconut branch were used. This makeshift version of the game was very popular, not only amongst the natives but also with the English tourists.

Playing cricket the way we did in Barbados helped the Island to produced some of the world's most prolific players. This was because of the surfaces we played on and also due to the confined spaces and the public roads on which we played.
In order for the batsman to get any substantial amount of runs, he had to place the ball meticulously along the ground in order not to be given out by hitting it onto the neighbour's house which often caused the irate neighbour to confiscate the ball or rush out of the house complaining. Normally by the time the neighbour appeared, everyone else had disappeared. The batsman also had to avoid being caught off the first bounce of the ball. The wicket generally consisted of two rocks placed about two feet apart and the ball had to pass between these two rocks in order to be given out. Naturally there were always arguments as to whether the ball did pass between the space made by the rocks or weather it had bounced too high over the wicket. There were, of course, those who never played the game in its true spirit and often caused controversy especially if they owned the bat or the ball. Everyone wanted to bat for as long as possible.

There was an abundance of many types of fresh fruit and sugar cane growing by the roadside and some neighbours gave freely. Those who were less than generous had to keep a constant watch on their mango and apple trees etc. to deter the boys and girls in the neighbourhood from feeding on their produce. Some of them would deliberately release their dog in the garden or purposely allow the dog to chase us down the street only to be met with a barrage of rocks.

Most Saturdays were taken up by attending the cinema to see the latest 'Roy Rogers' western in the mornings after Bible /conformation classes had finished and then hanging out (*liming*) in the city with friends to pass the time away. Sometimes in the evenings during the week, we would venture down to the local Pentecostal church to listen to the singing of the gospel hymns and watch in amazement as some of the congregation got into a frenzy whilst praying and singing. This show of Christian indulgence, although a very serious act of proclaiming allegiance to the Christian faith, provided a wealth of entertainment for us as children. We considered it better than attending a live performance in a theatre.

Sunday was specially reserved for church attendance which consisted of morning service, Sunday school in the afternoon followed by a stroll in the park, mainly to meet friends and generally enjoy ourselves with the fairer sex. This was then followed by evening service. But there was nothing more exhilarating than being chased by the local dogs which were unleashed when we patrolled the streets of our village in the late evenings either chatting up the girls or simply teasing the dogs and encouraging them to run after us.

Bank holidays were the days when groups of people got together for picnics on the beaches or excursions to local beauty spots where there would be fun and games and an abundance of food and drink which everyone shared. There was always the odd skirmish between boys which generally ended with the two opponents walking away with their arms around each other's shoulders, each one bragging that he was the more formidable opponent. Barbados was not an integrated society and although some of the white children on the island went to some of the same schools as the black children, that was as far as it went in terms of mixing and playing with each other.

The children are our future

School was very much disciplined. The correct uniform had to be worn and there was an inspection of the students for cleanliness every morning at primary school before the lessons started. Anyone contravening any of these very basic requirements was adequately punished. There was a well known saying that was rammed down our throats every morning (*Cleanliness is next to Godliness*) which stayed with me and no doubt, with the other students throughout our adult lives.

If a student was punished for any reason at school and this was later reported to his/her parents, that student would most likely be punished again by the parents for being punished at school in the first place. The method of punishment varied according to the severity of the deed committed. This included the boring and humiliating task of writing lines, (*writing one sentence repeatedly a considerable number of times promising not to commit the offence again)* being whipped with a leather strap by the teacher or the more shunned method of the cane administered by the head teacher across the buttocks or in the palm of the hand. Some students prepared for the cane by putting an exercise book in their trousers to reduce the pain felt but this often proved useless and the student would be given an extra lash for attempting such a deception.

Maintaining discipline and looking after the welfare of the children was every adult's responsibility. The able bodied adults also looked after the frail and elderly. In neither case it was not a requirement to be related. Caring enveloped the full circle from cradle to death. I remember being marched to school held by one ear by a neighbour after she caught me playing truant from school. This was the extent to which the adult neighbours cared about the welfare of the young children. Their future was to some extent dependent upon our success as adults although this was not the motive for their care and attention.

* * *

Throughout the past decades of the fifties and onwards, it was customary practice for the more affluent black parents in the English society to repatriate their children to their homeland to enjoy a better standard of life and primary and secondary education since the system in the UK did not cater fully for their children needs. This practice was more common among Barbadians and Jamaicans.

The West Indian culture is slightly different and our cultural strengths are based on what we have inherited from our African ancestry and Europeans during slavery and colonialism. Attitudes and behaviour of our children were often misinterpreted by English school teachers at large. Being black was perceived as an educational disadvantage and many black students were stereotyped as athletes or entertainers rather than individuals with academic ability. A bright, intelligent and assertive student was often portrayed as 'having a chip on his shoulder' or being arrogant and that unfortunate student would sometimes be demoted to a class well below his/her educational standard unless the parents were mindfully strong enough to intervene and stop the injustice which was rife throughout those decades.

The child's complaint to the parent nearly always resulted in the passive parent consoling the child and urging that child to do his best. In other words the child was being told; 'Think well of yourself and proclaim this fact to the world, not only in loud words but in great deeds.'

'Live in the faith that the whole world is on your side so long as you are true to do the best that is in you'.

These words were often not positive enough and was somehow encouraging that child to surrender his / her ideals and be submissive to racial injustice.

It did not seem to matter that the behavioural attitude of some of the school teachers was inadvertently damaging the personality of the some of the black children and as a result destroying their self esteem and denying them intellectual development which happened to be one of the debilitating components under the system of slavery when black people would be punished for attempting to educate themselves to an intellectually higher level.

The term **'uppity niggers'** *is still being used in to-day's civilised society.*

Some of the more intellectually aware West Indian parents saw a need to fill the void which was apparent in the English system of educating our children and found it necessary to give them extra tuition by establishing Saturday Schools in the predominately black communities which was generally staffed by black volunteer teachers and able parents. Those who were better off financially employed private tutors.

* * *

Vacancies in Barbados for good jobs in the nineteen fifties and sixties were few, hence everyone strived to achieve as good an education as they possibly could in order to be given consideration for a job in either the civil service, teaching at a primary school, working in a bank or getting an appointment with one of the more established companies on the island. Any positions higher than those mentioned required qualifications, such as a degree or the right colour of skin. It was highly competitive and all of the young men and women who were privileged to be educated at secondary school level expected just rewards for their achievements and so did their parents. Unfortunately, there were not enough jobs to go around for the indigenous young black educated young men and women.

I was educated at St. Giles Primary School in Saint Michael and then moved on to Combermere Secondary School where I finished my secondary education shortly before my eighteenth birthday. I entered the field of bookkeeping and worked for an established company in Barbados for the following two years before emigrating to England.

From an early age, (circa 12 years of age) I accompanied my father during the school holidays and at weekends on some of his many building construction jobs where I was taught the rudiments of the trade. It was then that I decided to pursue further education along this line and hence carve out a career for my future development. It occurred to me that the best way forward would be to travel to England and pursue the matter there because of the large range of vocational courses offered. Barbados was very limited in the number of courses offered along the lines of building/ engineering.

My life in Barbados was the best that I could have wished for but sacrifices had to be made in order that one may succeed in his determination to graze on greener pastures. I had visions of becoming an engineer. It did not matter whether it was Civil, Mechanical or Electrical.

Recruitment of young men and women for jobs in England was taking place at the time. I was one of those black young men recruited by London Transport Board from Barbados in 1962 to work on the London buses and trains. Some of the young men were recruited into the British army. The young ladies were mainly employed in the nursing profession. It was noticeable that during this exodus of young men and women from Barbados, there were no white faces to be seen.

Could it be that their future was already secured because of their white skins?

CHAPTER 3

Black heroes ; A touch of reality with the English way of life.

It was my first journey in an airplane and the first time on leaving the island except for a short journey off shore in a fishing boat. I had set out with several others from Barbados to seek the greener pastures of England or 'the mother country' as it was fondly referred to by us. (*Colonists of the British West Indies.*) To many of us, it was a journey into the unknown, for the few things that we knew about England were gathered through 'hearsay' and by the study of the history and geography of The British Isles whilst at school as there were subjects on the curriculum.

Barbados was British ruled. The main schools had English appointed headmasters. The curriculum originated in England. The examinations taken were set by English institutions and therefore the emphasis was on England. Students of that era had very little information that related to their own Black Heroes. It was as though they were omitted from the history books and we were not privy to this information.

Millions of people throughout the world now depend on inventions from the minds of Black people. We were told of Lord Nelson, Christopher Columbus, Abraham Lincoln, Benjamin Franklyn, all of the kings and queens of England and so on but we were ignorant to the exploits of black people such as:

Imhotep : *The father of medicine, poet, astrologer, the first universal scholar, architect, engineer and sage. He was recognised as the world's first doctor.*

Dr. Charles Drew *who discovered techniques to store blood and consequently developed blood banks*

Daniel Hale Williams – *the first successful heart surgeon and also created the first nursing school for black people in America.*

Elijah Mckoy (the real Mckoy): *An engineer who invented automatic lubrication systems for manufacturing machinery. This helped to increase production by allowing the machinery to work continuously for longer periods without having to shut down for routine maintenance.*

Garret Morgan *who invented the gas mask and traffic signals. It is ironic that Morgan had to employ the services of a white man to demonstrate his invention (gas mask) in the deep south of America so as to hide his racial identity. However as soon as this became known, orders for his invention stopped. His later invention (traffic signals) was sold to General Electrics and is now used world wide.*

Lewis Latimer. *The inventor of the carbon filament for light bulbs. His brilliance shone and the Lewis H Latimer school in Brooklyn, New York was dedicated to his memory*

Granville T. Woods : *Invented the Synchronous Multiplex Railway Telegraph for the purpose of train to station communication and thus avoiding accidents. He also pioneered the steam boiler furnace and the automatic air brake.*

Otis Boykin *invented the electronic control device for guided missiles, computers and the pace maker.*

Mary Seacole: *The Jamaican nurse who helped the British soldiers during the Crimean war.*

George Washington Carver – *Was dubbed one of the greatest scientist of all time. It was said that Carver's discoveries knew no limits. Although wilfully discriminated against, he never allowed himself to hate and worked selflessly with devotion to a life of service to mankind. He refused to accept money for any of his discoveries and often used what little he had to fund the education of both black and white students who fell on hard times.*

Alexander Mills *who invented the elevator….. The list goes on…….*

All of the above played a very significant part in the advancement of humanity and the modern society. The contribution to science and inventions by black people is so extensive that it is not possible to live a full day in any part of the world without sharing the benefits of their contribution. Yet their genius is generally unknown.
(The Ideology of Racism)

Cultural history and family values help to carve the inner fabric of one's existence in a society fraught with the dangers of racism and uncertainty. The deliberate omission of one's heritage leaves the recipient void and powerless to assert any dominance in the fight for equality.

* * *

My baptism into the English society.

I had expected the weather to be cold, but on that morning of 11th. January 1962, it was extremely cold with temperatures below freezing, "colder than usual," we were told. The howling icy winds that greeted us as we disembarked from the aircraft seemed to be saying 'NOT WELCOME' –go back to your Tropical Paradise of Barbados. Most of us wanted the pilot to turn around and take us back home. I asked myself. How can people possibly survive in these conditions? We took our fine weather and effortless existence in Barbados for granted.

You never miss the water until the well runs dry.

We had just arrived in England and were driven through some streets with some very unfamiliar looking buildings. What we thought to be one house was in fact a number of individual houses joined together. This seemed rather strange as the houses in Barbados were all individual dwellings with pockets of land separating each house. One person commented that his father owned a house and was amazed at the size of the houses only to realise afterwards that what he was witnessing was a number of small dwellings joined together.

We were awoken early the next morning in order to take a tour of London on an extremely cold and windy bus. The temperature as I recall was below freezing. Having just arrived from temperatures in the high eighties, this was a severe shock to the system. That morning we wore practically every piece of clothing we owned in order to keep warm. That well known saying 'Freeze your bollocks off' was often prevalent in my mind. I thought ; there is some truth in this saying after all.

We fully expected our pee to freeze before it hit the ground.

To me, London portrayed the likes of a gloomy and miserable place. It is a possibility that the driver of our tour bus excluded the livelier and more affluent parts of London. But on reflection, it was a dreadfully cold day. There was fog and therefore most people would have been at work or may have stayed indoors huddled in front of their coal fires or paraffin heaters; either of which constituted a health hazard in respect of their intake of oxygen along with the risk of fire.

These methods of heating were soon to be made obsolete or even outlawed because of the risks they posed mainly to the lives of children and the elderly. The combination of thick black smoke from chimneys and the fog formed the deadly mixture of 'smog' which caused respiratory problems and sometimes led to the death mainly of the frail and elderly. Some of the more fortunate were lucky to acquire accommodation which had gas fires and hot water boilers installed.

Central heating was a luxury only the rich could afford. Other than that, we used gas or electric fires. The gas and electric meters were coin operated and the price of these was set by the landlord which often meant an added charge to the already excessively high rent which was being paid to these greedy landlords who, unfortunately included some of my fellow Barbadians, some of whom were charged with the responsibility of getting us settled in our new environment.

Everyone seemed to be 'taking us for a ride' and our many protests fell on deaf ears. We had little alternative and therefore had to pay up for fear of being thrown out in the cold. Some of the lads unfortunately fell into this category and ended up spending the cold nights huddled in telephone kiosks trying to sleep while standing up. One of the lads reported that he was rescued from this terrible ordeal by an English woman who felt sorry for him and sneaked him into her home for warmth and shelter under the cover of darkness for fear of what her neighbours might say.

There was the case of my Jamaican friend who was married to a white Irish lady. One could only imagine the heartaches and insults they suffered in those early days. The wife was forced to deceive the landlord and sneaked her black husband into the house at night under the cover of darkness. Racism was not always a mitigating factor with some of the English. It seemed that many people acted in this manner in order to 'go with the flow' and not upset their neighbours who may or may not have had racist tendencies.

It only takes one bad apple to spoil a barrel full

The majority of us were employed as bus conductors by the London Transport Board but we never for one moment, thought that we would have to walk in front of the bus in the middle of winter with a torch or a white cloth in order to guide the driver through thick fog. I often went to the wrong house thinking that I had arrived home simply because all of the houses along the road were of the same design and I could not see the house numbers from the road side because of the dense fog. Needless to say, I wore multiple layers of clothing and appeared to be much bigger than my actual size. No one questioned the mask worn to cover my nostrils and mouth which was necessary to stop the inhalation of the smog. When the cold wind was at its most severe, it felt as though I was walking naked through the streets.
There were times when the smog was particularly bad and it was difficult to see anyone who was only a few feet away from you.

Black people had even more problems seeing each other.

The winter of 1962/63 called for the utmost endurance. The severity of that winter tested my West Indian colleagues and me to the full. We were walking on frozen snow for approximately three months. So severe was that winter, that parts of the Thames river were frozen solid from one bank to the other and provided a thoroughfare for some of the more adventurous and foolhardy who risked their lives by walking across the frozen waters. I often wore multiple pairs of socks but my feet were still frozen solid and swollen with the added problem of chilblains.

(Persistent itching and swelling caused by the lack of blood flow to the toes).
Many remedies were offered for this ailment; the most bizarre of which
was to pee on your feet. So annoying and painful was this condition that
even the most bizarre of methods were used to get relief.

Smog was a big problem. It was a severe health hazard and was instrumental
in the death of many of the elderly along with hypothermia (*extreme
coldness of the body*) and carbon monoxide poisoning caused from the fumes
of paraffin heaters which provided the only source of heat for many.

"The sun in England is cold"

This was a phrase coined by one of the local characters (King Dyall) in
Barbados on a return trip from England after being invited to watch a test
match series between England and the West Indies.

I had always heard, that the temperature in England was likened to that
of a freezer and that it was cold although the sun was shining. What a
load of rubbish; was my reaction. How can the sun be shining and yet it is
cold? A little while after arriving in England, there was glorious sunshine.
I was full of excitement and foolishly ventured out wearing just a cotton
shirt. It was only then that I realised that there was some truth in what
'King Dyall' said.

"The sun in England is cold". I managed about half a dozen steps before
rushing back into the house to the laughter of my friends.

Being used to temperatures of between 85 to 90 degrees every day of the
year, I found it hard to understand how the Sun could be shining down
on you and yet you are shivering cold. However, I was soon to discover
that it was not only the sun that was cold. The welcome we received and
the atmosphere we perceived were hardly inspiring. It was as cold as the
weather itself. I felt that the only way I could be consoled and fulfil my
needs was to educate myself to a higher level and return to Barbados. I had
to achieve my goals **Against All Odds** despite the hardships, negativity
and racist attitudes that I would encounter throughout the subsequent
years.

CHAPTER 4

Being naïve ; discovering the inner feelings of the racist mind

Before leaving Barbados for England, I had gathered information about life in England. I had become curious as to how the temperature in England would affect me. I would open the refrigerator door and stand in front of it for a few minutes and even put my head in the freezing compartment to see whether or not I would be able to sustain the cold temperatures. That was the extent of my naivety. I did not take into account the fact that the rest of my body was exposed to tropical temperature outside of the refrigerator and that by putting my head into a freezer for a few minutes would not have made the slightest difference to my body temperature.

A similarity of the type of weather that greeted us on our arrival from Sunny Barbados in January 1962.

The thought of not being accepted did not occur to me. I had prepared myself for the cold weather but not for the hatred and bigotry that I was to experience.

The fierce weather conditions of the winters were nothing compared to the tirade of abuse, the racist comments, disrespect and animosity which were to come. Racism also existed in my native country of Barbados and in these modern times, some of the white people of Barbados still act in this manner. This sad fact was experienced on a recent trip to Barbados (2010) when my wife and I along with two close friends stopped for a rest while walking along the beach and were alarmed when a white man came onto his veranda which overlooked that part of the beach and shouted at us to move along while exaggerating this demand with an offensive wave of his arm and in the process, threatened us with his dog.
There is a government directive that there are to be no private beaches in Barbados and we therefore stood our ground in an act of defiance and the perpetrator retreated, so did his dog.
(another racist bully trying to make black people succumb to his demands)

This exasperating and bigoted act by this person brought me to the conclusion that racist behaviour in my beloved country was still very much an issue. Although some of the white people make it a point to impress upon us that they are not of that calibre, there still exist an element of mistrust of white people primarily because of the behaviour of that un-enlightened few who seem to have retained their attitudinal DNA inborn into them from past colonial slave owners.

The white people of Barbados had the best houses, cars, jobs etc. There were certain prestigious positions earmarked for whites only and many of the blacks nationals had to settle for second best. The school you attended often played a great part in the job you were offered. If one did not do well at school, your immediate future depended on who your parents were or who they knew. This was not the case for your fellow white student who did not achieve academically as high as his fellow blacks student.

It was a very rare occasion to see a black person exposed to the public in a major bank or 'up-market' store in Barbados but never in my wildest dreams did I think that racism could be so venomously and blatantly administered as it was in England.

I immediately questioned my sanity but decided that I had little choice in the predicament in which I had placed myself. But I had to fulfil my dreams.

As a young man in Barbados, I was intrigued with the prospect of coming to England and getting some of that gold which supposedly paved the streets of London but unfortunately, someone had mistaken the colour of snow for the colour of gold.

Christianity proclaimed that "all men are created equal" but the deeds of its adherents spoke louder than their words and were proclaiming that white people are more equal than black people. The constitution and the laws were proclaiming equality for all men, whilst the enforcement of the law, respect for human rights, privileges, opportunities and responsibilities depended on the colour of one's skin.

CHAPTER 5

The wisdom of my parents and extended family; My Baptism.

They called her Dinky

I never found out why. My mother was a great lady and my hero. She was respected and loved by the hundreds of people whose lives she touched as well as those who knew her or knew of her. She was like a heavenly saint who would give her last penny to help a sinking soul. I remember how she quoted verses from The Bible either to put us on the correct path or to pacify us when we were sad. I will always remember her words to my brother when he complained that someone had told a lie about him. "Boy", she said. "They talked about Jesus, who do you think you are"

These words echo in my head every time I hear that some one has been spreading malicious gossip about me. Lies and gossip can easily destroy the human mind and cause animosity and hatred among individuals and even whole communities. I therefore got into the habit of ignoring gossip and taking a positive approach to let the gossipers realise that their dirty work was in vain.

My mother taught us to use the gifts that God gave us. I developed my quality of life by using my God given gifts of choice and intellect.
Self empowerment with meaningful intension and the will to do good by others were lessons never forgotten. "Love and trust in God", she would say. I later learnt more valuable lessons through experience as I got older.

The great lady eventually emigrated to the USA in order to get a better education for herself and also to help support her children and extended family more effectively. She studied early childhood education and was subsequently awarded a Degree. She went on to teach at a primary school in New York after claiming that she was five years younger in order to secure the job. Consequently she had to work an extra five years before she could officially retire. The job was never a strain on her and she also enjoyed every day of that extra time with her students. She was a successful entrepreneur while she resided in Barbados and continued to work with those skills in New York to provide extra income for her family.

My mother eventually purchased a house in New York and made plans for all of her children to join her. Sadly, this was not to be and my three sisters were the only ones to take up the offer. My youngest brother remained in Barbados to carve out a career for himself while two other brothers and I adopted England as our home. Her grandchildren were later to benefit mostly from her efforts. There was one grandson (*Dr. Kurt Lambert*) who made her and the rest of the family extremely proud of his achievements over the years by gaining his PhD in Economics at a very early age and has since been appointed to the board of directors of the London Stock Exchange after starting his own successful investment business in Switzerland despite the many obstacles and hardships and his humble upbringing in Carrington Village, Barbados.

It turned out that my mother (*Dinky – as she was affectionately known*) was the first port of call for many 'Bajans' (*citizens of Barbados*) entering New York who found themselves stranded with nowhere to live. She would always give them temporary shelter (*without monitory gain*) and help them on their way.
She was later publicly awarded for her help and generosity to the immigrants to New York who arrived homeless from Barbados. It would appear that her New York address was passed around to people intended on going to New York to seek prosperity.

Dinky (Stacie) later died (age 82) in the most tragic accident in which part of her home was consumed by fire and she was unable to escape despite the efforts of my youngest sister who was with her at that unforgettable moment in our lives. My sister was badly burnt and still has the scares etched on her mind and body.

The house has since been restored and her presence and love remain in the building. An estimated 2000 people attended her funeral. The mourners arrived from Canada, Barbados, Switzerland and England as well as neighbouring states in America. The funeral was officiated by 3 Anglican priests (*one of whom was her cousin who travelled from the neighbouring Canada.*) at St.Cryprians Church, Brooklyn, New York. The officiating clergy anticipated a large gathering and were adequately prepared with extra seats and loud speakers placed in the church car park in order to allow the over-spill to follow the service. Such was her popularity among the New Yorkers and others. She is remembered for her good deeds and a stair lift partly donated and inspired by her for the elderly, stands in her memory at the church where she worshiped.

These are the words inspired by her and have served me well.

Control your thoughts. Your thoughts become your words.....

Control your habits. Your habits become your destiny..........

Thoughts follow words. Words follow thoughts...............

It does not matter what you think...control what you do.......

Be motivated by the spirit of God.......

Everything we do is resident in our choice.......

Use your life as a powerful and helpful source to help others.

* * *

He was affectionately known as 'Dagan'

My father was a brilliant and thoughtful man. He was a planner and had the foresight that that most people of that era lacked. He had several children (*not of the same mother*) and was proud of each one of us. Despite the fact that there were so many, this never deterred him from accepting his responsibilities and showing his commitment to each of us. We were educated by him at the 'University of life' and to the highest standards at secondary school according to our individual abilities. He taught us how to survive with what little we had. One of his many talents was the art of improvising.

I recall one of our weekly journeys home after cultivating some of his agricultural land far away in the rural part of Barbados. We were unfortunate to sustain a punctured tyre. There was no spare wheel to fall back on. My father promptly sent me into the field to cut some grass while he removed the affected wheel. This puzzled me far a while.

He then proceeded to remove the inner tyre and filled the vacant space of the outer tyre with the grass. He then replaced the grass filled wheel and got us safely home. Such was his ingenuity. He often said to me 'one hundred cents make one dollar' implying that nothing should be wasted and we should make use of everything we have.

We were encouraged to be thrifty and creative with the little resources we had available to us. Carving toys out of scraps of wood, making scooters by using discarded ball bearings as wheels was an everyday occurrence. We had to make our own cricket bats and used anything that was remotely round as a ball in order to complete the set. We often made cricket balls from discarded tennis balls by heavily wrapping them with tape or we would manufacture a cricket balls by soaking newspaper, wrapping it with pieces of cloths and then binding the two together by knitting a secure web around them with cord.

Our education also involved private tuition when it was necessary to supplement our primary or secondary education. The majority of my brothers and sisters were fortunate to secure scholarships to attain a secondary education and this lessened the burden of paying school fees which were mandatory at the time.

(*During the mid 1960's, every child was given the right to free secondary education in Barbados by the Government under the leadership of Rt. Hon. Errol Barrow*) 'Dagan', as most people referred to him, had his own successful business as a building contractor – a skill which he learnt and perfected while living in Cuba and was the first man to design and build the traditional style bungalow which was soon to be copied by many in Barbados.

This unique design (*as it was then*) brought him popularity as a builder and thus his order book was always full. I learnt many of my design, planning and building skills from him and thus immigrated to England with a view of expanding that knowledge and returning home to join him and eventually take over the business. Unfortunately, this was not to be.

* * *

My oldest brother was my inspiration and role model during the short time that we were domicile here. He arrived in England approx 4 years before I did. He, along with two older sisters, an older brother and an uncle were my main sources of information, guidance and support. I was more fortunate than others to have close members of my family residing in England who were ready and able to educate me in the arts of 'survival' in my new 'neighbourhood'.

They were to be invaluable in my 'baptism' to the English society and also gave valuable advice and guidance to my close friends who were also new to the country and were eager to listen and learn. Before my arrival in England, my brother had achieved his goal in becoming a barrister and was making plans to return home to Barbados.

Because of his new role, it was necessary for him to be an inspirational speaker and he often practiced his public speaking on Sunday mornings at 'Speakers corner' in Hyde Park, London, along with other aspiring barristers, politicians and generally, those who had something to say.

Unfortunately, this public platform was often taken advantage of and indiscriminately and maliciously used by bigots and zealots of every description who cowardly stood on their 'soap boxes' and took advantage of the 'freedom of speech' to slander, abuse and ridicule others irrespective of whether it was religious, political, personal or racial.

Was this what the English Society was about?

I realise that freedom of speech is one of the main instruments of a democratic society but Sunday Mornings at Speaker's corner was exceptional in that anything could be said without fear of prosecution. As a new resident in London and coming from a country where we were taught to love and respect our fellow man, I was surprised and appalled at the behaviour that I was witnessing in this civilised society and yet our style of life and our culture was being questioned by some of these same people.

CHAPTER 6

Humiliation and degradation; The fight for recognition understanding and equality.

Struggling to keep warm had no racist connotations. But somehow it appeared that we as black people suffered more than our white neighbours in this endeavour. There were feelings of anger and oppression. We were ushered into substandard housing, often in a state of disrepair and draughty with mouldy walls and surrounding dampness. Young children and the elderly were mostly at risk from these conditions.

Better housing was often available to rent, but notices were indiscriminately posted stating;

'NO BLACKS'
'NO IRISH'
'NO DOGS'

One can only imagine the humiliation, anger and disgust that was felt after being put in the same category as dogs and knowing that our English hosts did not want us sharing their space…. Indoors or out…. Some of them found it difficult to see beyond slavery or the colour of our skin. Crude remarks like "Go back where you came from" or sounds imitating monkeys were an everyday occurrence.

Was this some form of legalised discrimination?

I ask the question simply because this abominable behaviour was being ignored by the authorities and law makers of the day. The value of humanity, the right to freedom, justice and liberty were not yet on the agenda of the British politicians. Not much consideration was given to our basic human rights. We were emigrant workers and should have been eternally grateful for the opportunity to live and work in this country under any condition imposed upon us.

Or should we???

There was inherent determination in the minds of some, that black people be kept to near slavery conditions as possible and we were evaluated on the basis of our skin colour.

This racist behaviour towards black people puzzled me for a while. I could not understand why it was so aggressively portrayed and administered with such venom because English people are always welcomed in Barbados and the rest of the Caribbean and are treated with kindness and respect and one had hoped that this warm welcome and respect would have been reciprocated. It seemed as though some of the English visitors to the shores of Barbados expected this warm welcome purely because of their white skins and the feelings of superiority in a 'black' environment.

During the era of the sixties and seventies, the French authorities also appeared to be on the bandwagon. Black people travelling from England to Calais on daily shopping trips were often singled out and harassed by the French police and French custom officers of the day. Protests were duly made when a coach load of Black shoppers travelled to France specifically for the purpose of confronting the French authorities. They were led by a black counsellor on behalf of the Black community as the French attitude against black visitors became apparent. Little was done to appease the disgruntled protesters as they were politely ushered through customs and ignored by the police who it seemed, did not want to create an international incident.

I must stress that racist attitudes were not always seen to be present in the minds of the more enlightened people of the English society. A great number were curious about these black people who had invaded their space and wanted to learn more about us since we seemed to know much more about them than they knew about us.
We took it upon ourselves to study the history, geography and culture of the English so that there would be little difficulty in blending into a society in which we had planned to spend a number of years of our lives.

Barbados has a parliament similar to that of Westminster. The Nelson statute was erected in Trafalgar Square in Barbados before it was erected in Trafalgar square, London. The history of England and the British Empire was part of the curriculum taught in our schools.

In the search for better housing in those days, it would either be a blatantly racist sign to deter your application or somehow the room / flat you were hoping to rent was 'just taken' only to find that this really wasn't the case, because you would send a trusted white friend to apply for the same room /flat only to find that the room/flat was in fact still vacant and available to your white friend.

I recall one such occasion where I knocked on a door after seeing the 'room for rent' sign. A white lady answered the door and was pleased to inform me that the room was still available. A white male, on seeing me, hastily approached the front door only to inform me that the room had been taken minutes before I had arrived. The lady was clearly embarrassed and apologised. Naturally I ask my white friend to apply and not surprisingly, he was offered the room.

* * *

Some white males seemed to have had a fear of black males living under the same roof as their wives/girlfriends. It was apparently this myth about black men and sex that bothered them. On the other hand, some English people simply could not bear the thought of having a black neighbour or black house mate. After all, what would the neighbours say?

Somehow the deplorable conditions and racist attitudes strengthened my will and determination. I did not have the funds to return to Barbados and was not inclined to do so without some credence of my ability in building design after having been taught the basics by my father. Some of my friends enlisted the help of their family and decided to return to Barbados only after a short stay.

I was here to fight with every ounce of my being for a better place in this society and hence a better and more rewarding job. Life was tough financially and otherwise. I was paying back a loan that I had from the Barbados Government for my air fare and at the same time I had to pay extortionate sums of money for rent and food. We were naive and as a result, exploited by some of our own countrymen along with others. We were forced to share a small room with as many as five others and paid half of our wages to these people who were supposed to be helping us. The rent supposedly included meals but because of the shift work, we were lucky to get a meal. This meant paying for meals we never had and at the same time, having to purchase food elsewhere.

Some restaurants refused to serve us. If we were lucky to be served, we were expected to leave as soon as we had finished our meal. Sometimes a staff member would take up a position at the door when we were near the end of our meal, presumably to stop us if we decided to leave before paying. Browsing around stores often turned out to be insulting and degrading. At times the store assistants would blatantly follow us around giving the impression that we were thieves and had to be carefully watched. Whilst browsing around a store, you would be constantly asked by the store assistant if you required any help. Although some of them genuinely wanted to help if you showed some uncertainty of what you wanted to purchase, the majority were there simply to keep an eye on us.

* * *

It was soon apparent that our naivety and inexperience of being newly appointed London Transport Board employees was also being exploited by some of the managers /inspectors whose sole purpose it seemed, was to use us as fodder to booster themselves in the eyes of their superiors.

I was somewhat lucky in being paired off with a young English white male bus driver who made me aware of what went on in the industry. He turned out to be my first real friend in England. Such was his loyalty and trust in me that he persuaded his father to sign a hire purchase agreement on my behalf after knowing me for only three months. It was then that I realised that a person should always be judged by his ethics and behaviour rather than his external appearance and that it was wrong to stereotype, especially when it is negative. Much of my faith had been restored.

Because of the way we were treated in the early stages of our arrival in England, I was consumed with mistrust and was wary about every white person I had encountered. I never thought that an English person would have gone to that length for a black stranger whom he had met only a short time before.

Black bus conductors would be reported for trivial matters and were sometimes under the threat of loosing their jobs. Insubordination was a common reason for being reported when we stood up to these racist bullies. This unscrupulous element of London Transport Board knew that they had us 'over a barrel' because of the difficulty in finding alternative employment in a market which was indiscriminately fraught with racism. Being watched and spied on by our supervisors was one of those things we had to endure on a daily basis.

CHAPTER 7

The perpetrators of racial violence in London; Hatred levied at the Black man; Using education as a viable means of equality and upholding the importance of culture.

I am very sceptical of media reporting and found it difficult to comprehend the reports as to the extent of the atrocities that were being committed on West Indians in England by the now infamous 'teddy boys' of London. I ask myself. Could this really have been true?

There were reports of a 'Keep Britain White' campaign led by a British titled politician : Sir Oswald Mosely who formed the British Union of Fascists movement which incited racial hatred and created a considerable amount of tension in society resulting in psychological, social and economic issues.

Was there such a large cultural division between the West Indian and the English people ? Why did it lead to such violent encounters?

These questions puzzled me for a while and I soon realised that it was the colour of our skin and not our culture that was the cause of such fierce confrontations which were partially quelled when a group of West Indians, mainly Jamaicans, decided to fight back in order to preserve and demand their right to live peacefully and with due respect in this land. The turning point of the violent encounters (*The Notting Hill Riots*) was the attendance of approximately twelve hundred people, both Black and White to the funeral of a black man who was brutally attacked and stabbed to death by a gang of white youths. There was a feeling of solidarity and common support for the grieving family. Two people came together as one because of this tragic incident.

Decades later, there was to be a similar incident in which a Black youth *(Stephen Lawrence)* was set upon and brutally stabbed to death by a gang of White youths. This incident also captured the solidarity of the nation and the police are still pursuing methods such as the repealing of the Double Jeopardy Law in an effort to bring the allegedly known murderers to justice.

It is ironic that such a fierce episode of violence should generate that measure of respect which we as black people now command in England. One could liken this to the atrocities of both ancient and modern times when countries fought their aggressors in order to get recognition, peace and independence for themselves and for future generations. It is my belief that the 'Notting Hill' riots of the late fifties were instrumental in much of the eradication of racial violence in London.

Bullies often back down when the challenge is accepted.

It is also ironic that the same measure of respect demanded by black people of that era is now being used as a build up to violent acts on the streets by some of the black youths of today's generation. *(circa 2000/2010)*. It seems that we no longer enjoy the extended family structure and it is now left to the wider society to draw on the positive aspects of our culture and instil in the youth, sound values such as respect, honesty, diligence, hard work, courage, tolerance, fairness and patriotism to ensure future success.

Revisiting these values would also ensure that the black youths of today would be able to fulfil the potential and responsibility they have to themselves, the community, their country and also to be treated as entire citizens of a society into which they were born.

What you do is a big part of who you are. Black youths should educate themselves with accurate information about the people of the African Diaspora in order draw inspiration from their struggle and journey through slavery and not to see themselves as underachievers and show pride in the way our ancestors were able to contribute in a major way to the development and transformation of many countries throughout the world.

One would now ask the question, why have so many black youths become persona non grata?

There could be many answers but until we know why, it would not be possible to reach any plausible solutions. Peer pressure seems to be one of the main reasons and experience has shown that this can be eradicated by persistently vigilant parents who transmit to their children and other young people the core values of good manners, honesty, integrity, and discipline so as to combat the erosion of social values.

It has become for too easy to shift the blame to others (*ie. schools, friends, television programs, etc*).
Faith, hope and empowerment are three of the key features along with that most popular adage 'Prevention is better than cure' must constantly be bourn in mind in order to develop the character of our youths. They must get to know the power of God, and that He is there to guide them.

There is no need to take 'coke'. There is always hope.

They must be aware of the best they can be and develop purity of motion and thought, strength of mind and integrity and proceed to move forward. We have, over the years, neglected to discipline our children and called it self esteem; but at what cost?

Many black youths seem to develop abject personalities from an early age in this racially charged society. Whether at home, in the classroom or the playground, attention is sought by some means or other and if one means of attention is not forthcoming, then another is sought and so on.
In many cases, recognition and attention are the main criteria: Someone to talk to…. ..someone to listen…….some place to belong….. etc.

Cultural penetration has led to moral decay in the society where people no longer make a distinction between what is right and wrong and show gross disrespect for law and order.
In the minds of many youths, it does not seem to matter whether the activity is legal or illegal as long as they can relate to or can be noticed and applauded by their peer group. For this reason, negative peer culture must be eliminated.

* * *

We did not have television in Barbados and relied solely on other peoples' (*newspaper reporters*) versions of what was happening in 'The Mother

Country' to our black brothers and sisters. After all, we are a British colony and we were invited by the British Government to fill the voids in certain areas of employment. Barbadians are a proud people and this pride is based on our perception of ourselves that we are educated, intelligent, resilient and sociable.

Promises of employment from the English employers and the British Government started an exodus of labour from the Barbados and other neighbouring British Commonwealth countries of the Caribbean. Many young men and women with high standards of education left their prospective countries because of the employment promises and also the opportunities that were available to further their education and improve the standard of life for themselves and the families back home that would come to rely on them in future years. We were looked upon as ambassadors for our countries. Little did we realise that economic growth and success of our countries would be partly dependent on our own individual success in this foreign land.

Somehow, there was a sense of black people being classed as somewhat inferior and uncivilised which allowed the rich world to go on exploiting and plundering the natural and human resources to help finance industrial growth in the larger and more developed nations. Everybody made money out of the black people -- landlords through exploitation -- employers through inadequate wages and the government through taxes.

The input of the black workers was crucial, especially to the Health Care services, the transport industry, the armed forces and some of the manufacturing industries. There was a desperate shortage of manpower in Great Britain and the people of the Caribbean were short of work. It was an exchange of prosperity for all parties concerned although, one may add, some prospered more that others.

The British economy grew stronger, the problems of employment for young people in the Caribbean had eased and the emigrants were now in a better financial position to support their families back home with foreign currency which also meant economic growth for the islands in the Caribbean. Our ambassadorships also helped immensely in the tourist industry.

The qualifications which were taken to England by the migrant workers from the Caribbean were irrefutable and could not be challenged as being of a lower standard because they were exactly the same examinations (*The Oxford and Cambridge General Certificate of Education*) which were taken by our English counterparts. Contrary to the beliefs of some of the English employers, race does not predict academic standards. The people of the Caribbean took a certain pride in their respective islands and strived to maintain a high standard of education because this was the only road to success and prosperity for the majority of all concerned. There was a duplication of standards in the Caribbean with that of England in almost every aspect of education and governance. The British Government ensured that their colonies in the West Indies adhered to the rules and acts of the British Parliament.

Although there were democratically elected members of the parliaments in the Caribbean Islands, power was somewhat limited and legislation had to be ratified by the British Parliament through their representative - The Governor. When independence was eventually gained by the majority of the British Commonwealth Islands in the Caribbean, the highest court of appeal (*The Privy Council*) remained in the jurisdiction of the British Government.

The meeting Place for MP's: The House of Assembly in Barbados

View of the Careenage next to the House of Assembly in Barbados

It was inevitable that these well educated young men and women would seek better paid employment to match their qualifications and ambitions. They were not going to be held back. Competition with the indigenous white applicant for a better paid position nearly always resulted in the white person being preferred. Sometimes the fact that the white person was less qualified did not enter into the equation and in order to ensure that we as black people were above the standards required for the positions applied for, we sought to acquire higher levels of qualifications in order to be more competitive.

These higher qualifications sometimes presented the added problems of being 'over qualified' for the position applied for. There were always excuses or insipid explanations to stop black people from achieving their full potential. It was like a plot to brainwash black people into believing that they were only good for the menial downgraded positions which carried little scope of prospect for promotion and paid very little wages. We were being held by this massive invisible force which seemed impenetrable. It was tantamount to legalised discrimination. It is my belief that the employers somehow underrated their black employees and overlooked the possibility of having 'Black' managers in their organisations. They were not adequately prepared for this influx of new multi-talented people and reacted with prejudice and indifference.

At last, 'a ray of hope'.

It seemed as though the London Transport Board was finally beginning to recognise the potential of some of its black workers. We no longer lived in a world of complete hopelessness and were gradually made aware of the various avenues that were available in order to advance beyond our present positions. I personally decided to enrol for the special London Transport course at a local college with a view of getting promotion but after a short attendance I realised that the course seemed to have been created mainly for the black employees and it would seem that this was a concerted effort by the employers to give us a false impression that this ill designed and badly administered course was the first step in preparing us for promotion in the industry. Many of the students withdrew from the course after a short while.

The course content seemed like an insult to our education and intelligence and was regarded as sub-standard rubbish and a waste of time by the majority of those who attended. It was seen as an attempt to divert attention from the real issues of the day and used as a smoke screen by the London Transport Board to give the impression that they were addressing the issues which confronted them. I resisted the temptation to further myself in this industry as it would have been an unsatisfactory diversion.

Despite the academic ability of some Caribbean applicants when competing for positions with their white counterparts, there were always feeble excuses as to why the 'Black' applicant did not get the position or even reached the interview stage. I can recall being invited to attend interviews which never happened. The prospective employers would offer excuses but the obvious reason for rejection without even an interview, was the colour of my skin and there was nothing that I could do about it. These rejections, although designed to deter black applicants, made us more determined to challenge the system.

The non-admission of racism by employers seemed to have been countered when application forms started to appear with a separate section where the applicants had to state their ethnicity. It was claimed that this information was for statistical purposes. That may have been true but the consensus of opinion was that this method was being used by most employers to eliminate black applicants from the onset.

Legislation was not yet in place to challenge this outlandish and racial behaviour. On the other hand, it should not have to take an act of parliament to stop racism. The only way to stop this deplorable behaviour is for the people concerned to stop hating and the hating often occur without a reasonable cause. In any case, legislation is powerless to eradicate racial instincts or to abolish distinctions based upon physical differences.

I was once taken to a large office before a pre-arranged interview was to have been conducted. The prospective interviewer said to me. "Look around you". The interviewer was obviously telling me that I would not fit into the environment to which he had introduced me. I was being judged on the colour of my skin and not on my ability to do the job. There was a 'sea' of white faces in the office. I never got the interview despite being told in the reply to my written application that my qualification was acceptable. Nothing was portrayed of the racist behaviour of this multi-national company in their advertisement to recruit personnel… a company which benefited from contracts with many Black nations through-out the world.

Employment selection criteria are piously claimed to be determined purely by merit and ability to do the job. In practice, application forms from black people are thought to be screwed up and consigned to the rubbish bins.

In order to gain employment which was commensurate with qualifications in one of the more recognised companies, black applicants would often use part of their true qualification to get in on the ground floor. After they had established themselves, they would then reveal the full range of their qualifications and expertise in order to gain the position they wanted in the first place. This method was preferred as it often yielded the desired results. The theory was that the employer would have time to assess them after time spent in the lower position and not judge them for the higher position in the first instance when they most probably would have been rejected.

The planned five years term in which I would get better qualification and gather enough experience in order to return to Barbados had to be put on hold. Attitudes, ignorance and the fear of the unknown held by some of the indigenous population created huge barriers

CHAPTER 8

Christianity and the West Indies dominance of World cricket.

We are a Christian people, indoctrinated mainly into the Anglican and Catholic faiths by English priest or English trained priests in the West Indies. Many of us sought solace in churches of the same denomination as we attended in the West Indies but after comparing notes with others, we reached the same conclusion. We felt that we were not wanted, neither as worshipers in the church nor as residents in the country.

One of the most alarming experiences was with my friend who I will refer to as LB. He said that after the service in this popular Anglican Church, the priest went to the door, as is customary to greet his congregation. LB said that he was held back and then politely told by the priest that he was most welcome but he did not think that the congregation was happy to have him there and asked him not to return. This appalling behaviour was not uncommon in churches during that era and the behaviour experienced by LB was also experienced by other West Indians.

I beg the question:
Were the priest who indulged in this unsocial and unchristian behaviour really speaking on behalf of the congregation or were they trying to use the 'so called' will of the congregation as an excuse to reflect their own feelings?

The word soon spread among black people and action had to be taken. It was unfortunate that some of the English churches had their reputations damaged by a few bigoted priests who were not worthy of the positions they held.

Black church goers needed somewhere to congregate and worship in a friendly atmosphere which was conducive to the joy and fulfilment of prayer. Pentecostal churches catering mainly for black people became increasingly popular and attracted huge numbers of people who had decided to change from the traditional Anglican and Catholic faiths in order to meet their needs. This method of worship was found to be joyful and full of life and excitement and was frowned upon by some of the more traditional churches throughout England but their objections to this type of worship fell on deaf ears and small numbers of dissatisfied white worshipers also started drifting into the Pentecostal churches.

It was noticed that in recent years, some of the English churches gradually changed their practices of worship and adopted a more light-hearted and livelier approach to their programme as if to woo the congregation back.

Cricket *lovely* cricket

Little by little the barriers were broken down by a common sense approach and sport. We took advantage of our ability to play sport well, especially cricket and were soon to be the toast of the London Transport Board and any other club that might have employed our services at the time. We not only showed that we played well in team sport and acted in unison with other employees but we also supported each other in matters concerning our welfare. We were a fully united body and sent a clear signal. We were recognised for our tact and diplomacy in handling sensitive matters and above all, winning cricketing awards for the clubs concerned.

West Indies cricket was at its highest level. We conquered the world and were 'unbeatable' for a considerable number of years. This gave us a sense of pride and we held our heads high. We were recognised as the best in the world. No one could take that away from us. We therefore used our cricketing skills to infiltrate and break down some of the social barriers. The success of our cricket team played a big part in our climb to social acceptance in the English society. Village and county teams drew larger crowds simply because West Indian cricketers were playing. It did not matter that we were not the actual test players. The fact remained that we were West Indians, the flamboyant stars of the cricketing fraternity and we were expected to entertain. After all, we were the world's best and were expected to perform well above the usual standards weather or not we played in the test arenas on the hallow turf of Lords or the Oval.

Our pride was at its highest when the West Indian team played in England. The games played at Lords and the Oval cricket were always the highlight of the tour and attracted thousands of loyal followers from all over England. Employers expected most of their West Indian workers to be 'sick' during those times. It was the creed of every West Indian cricketing fan to attend at least one game. I would arrive at Lords or the Oval cricket ground sometimes as early as five o'clock so as to be one of the first to be in the queue for tickets, only to find that I had approximately three to four hundred people in front of me, mainly West Indians.

Arriving after all of the tickets were sold presented little problem as tickets stubs were sent over the wall or some one would collect them from friends on the inside, come out of the ground with the intention of returning and distribute the tickets stubs to waiting friends who would simply show them and walk into the grounds without being challenged. The only disadvantage of this method was that we missed a part or all of the first session of the game but that didn't matter as long as we saw our stars performing.

Somehow the expectations of our performance reminded me of the days of segregation in America when the only way a black person would be admitted to a renowned venue was because he/she was a good artiste and his/her job was primarily to entertain the more affluent whites customers.

Apartheid was prominent in South Africa and their sports men and women (black and white) could not compete together or against each other. Neither were they given the chance to compete internationally despite the efforts of the other nations to persuade the government to exclude sport from its deplorable practices.

Sport was seen in the eyes of many as a plausible means of integrating the races of South Africa since every other diplomatic effort failed to sway the consciences of the leaders. Nelson Mandela (*who later became president of South Africa*) was held prisoner because of his objections to this unfair and inhumane practice. Rhodesia under the premiership of Ian Smith was trying to adopt the same principle and this seemed to have had some effect on the way some of the English people were behaving towards the Black community. Thankfully the Rhodesian government was persuaded from adopting this practice by the British parliament.

The English politicians were debating the repatriation of black immigrants from the Caribbean. Many of us were of the opinion that we would have been forced to leave England. There was pandemonium in the minds of many black immigrants which was exacerbated by the behaviour of extremist political groups which, as it seemed, were formed mainly to oppose the presence of black people in this country.

The infamous the 'Rivers of blood speech' was given by the renowned Tory politician Enoch Powell in which he advocated that emigration should cease in order to stop; not only more Black people from entering the country but also to curtail the growth of those who were already here, since a considerable number of dependants of the existing emigrants were now being brought into the country. There was also much concern about the descendants swelling to an imaginable majority. Mr. Powell seemed to be of the opinion that Blacks would over-run the country and the 'fear' of this happening incited the English people to an extent of near political disorder.

The mere title of his speech gave people the impression that he was inciting race riots and this caused much fear and mistrust between Blacks and Whites, particularly in the areas of England where Black people were most visible.

Black Caribbean people were accused of taking the jobs from the English but these jobs were given to us simply because they themselves did not want them. If the English economy was to strive, then the work had to be done by someone. Hence the reason the British Government turned to nationals of the Caribbean to fill these voids. A large number of hopeful British Commonwealth immigrants came to England as full citizens and therefore had the rights of every other English citizen. Entry into England was alike an admission to privileges and opportunities eagerly sought after.

The impact on the existing population was immediate with regards to the reduction in school places, hospital admissions etc. for them. There was a fear among the English people that large scale immigration would bring increases in crime and that immigration was being used to change the social make up of the country. This was seen as a threat to the English people and may have incited more racial behaviour purely through fear and frustration at the loss of jobs to migrants and the pressure put on public services and social housing. Happily common sense won the day. There was a degree of tolerance and understanding shown by the English people after a period of uncertainty. Although some of the barriers were broken down, we still had a long way to go. But as the years rolled on and as we asserted ourselves, attitudes started to change for the betterment of all.

CHAPTER 9

Recognising the racist elements of the society and separating them from the genuine patriots.

I remained an employee of London Transport Board until January 1969. This was much longer than originally planned and was due to constant rejections for alternative employment and also the fact that by then my true goal seemed to be getting beyond reach. No company was willing to take me on and train me further in the art of Building Design. I had reached the age of 27 and time was fast running out.

My opportunity came purely by chance when I met a friend who had enrolled on a training course which was run by the Manpower Services Commission (M.S.C), (*a government backed institution which was set up to train people to work in the Engineering industry*).

I thought this was as close to my dream as I would get. It gave me the opportunity to get a base and lay a foundation for my future plans. I was always fascinated by people in any engineering discipline who had a series of professional qualifications and thought; one day I will have these credentials.

I applied the next day, passed the necessary test and was accepted for training. My goal was now within reach. The phrase that I often heard was now becoming a reality.
(***You can achieve whatever you want to achieve if you work hard enough for it***)
And again, to quote that famous phrase of President Barack Obama...
"YES WE CAN".

* * *

My Introduction to Engineering

I eagerly reported to the training centre at Wadden near Croydon, Surrey at 8 o'clock on a Monday morning in January 1969 to start training as a 'Capstan Setter Operator' I had no idea what the training entailed nor did I know what a Capstan was. All that I was concerned about was that it was mechanical engineering training and this would provide the basic training that I needed to get those credentials I longed to have.

I was greeted by my instructor: An Englishman, smartly dressed, approx 40 years old and wearing a white coat. I promptly enquired of him." Which of these machines is the capstan ?" He said , "They all are" , and gave me a rather strange look as if to say. 'What do I have here?' He then asked, to my astonishment.
"How many sixteenths are there in one inch?"
I became a bit curious as to why he would ask me a question with such an obvious answer. Does he think that I am stupid? On answering the question, I said, "Why did you ask me that?" He said, "You'd be surprise at the answers I get". The answer was not so obvious after all. He told me that he once asked a former trainee how many thousandths are there in one inch. The reply was, "there must be millions".

I successfully completed the course with about five weeks to spare, in which time I was able to infiltrate into other classes and gained some valuable knowledge and experience in the use of other types of mechanical production machinery. Under the supervision of my instructor, I was also helping to train others on this 'roll on, roll off' course which lasted a total of six months. It was an intensive course and attendance was required five days a week, eight hours a day. I admired and respected my instructor for the way he taught and advised me, not only in the tasks of manufacturing components but in the role of instructing others. He had become my role model and I soon realised that I was also the role model for some of the trainees *(both black and white)* who joined the course after I did. I was always willing to share what knowledge I had gained with them.
This was a prelude to my intended career.
I soon realised that the other trainees respected me mainly for what I knew and was able to pass on to them. The colour of my skin did not matter.

I was brimming with confidence and felt that I could undertake any engineering production job successfully. This confidence was apparent to my first employer who advertised for an engineer with at least five years experience in the industry. Although I had not quite completed the full six months of my course, my instructor recommended me to the prospective employer for the post. He hired me and his confidence in me was soon to be realised in that he was ready to put me in a supervisory position at a new branch that he was about to open after only three months in his employ.

My job took me from my home in Teddington in Middlesex to Crawley in Sussex, a journey of about fifty miles. I decided to supplement my newly acquired skills with an evening course in an engineering discipline at Redhill College which happened to be on my way to and from work. I was joined by a West Indian friend (*who I will refer to as RT*) with whom I travelled and was also a former trainee.

After the first two weeks at college, I was singled out by the course tutor who happened to be English and was told that I was wasting my time on the general engineering course which I was studying and that I would be much better off doing the more advanced City & Guilds Engineering Technicians course. The most appropriate college happened to be Putney College in South West London approximately forty five miles from work and much nearer to my home.

I appreciated the foresight of this Lecturer and would be forever thankful to him for his advice and guidance.

In order to attend this course, It meant that I would have to resign my Job and seek employment nearer to my home West of London. I told my employer of my intention and he immediately offered me a rise in wages in order to deter me from leaving. He also provided travelling expenses for both my friend and I as I travelled in his car. He even offered to use his influence as an employer in the town to get me a priority placement on the Local Council's housing list. But my goal was now becoming a reality and nothing was going to stop me.

I could not abandon my goals for the sake of a few extra pounds and decided to follow my heart. My friend who lived in South London also resigned his post and we travelled together to Putney College to enrol for the recommended course. The course was in its second week but we had a good excuse for the late start and were willing to do the extra work in order to catch up.

* * *

A Sixth Sense

It was an imposing building and the place was abuzzed with learning activities. We were excited as we approach the reception where a young white woman was sitting at her desk. After greeting us with a rather pleasant smile, she announced to us that she was very sorry but the course we wanted to study was already fully subscribed and there was a waiting list. This woman did not check or even pretended to check but was somehow able to immediately inform us that the course was full. Our chances seemed doomed. But.....

Do you ever get that feeling that you are not being told the truth?

Well, I did, and my instincts were right. Previous encounters had taught me not to take everything or everyone at face value. I was suspicious and decided to check for myself.

Directly adjacent to the reception, the location of the classes was posted. My friend and I soon found the classroom where the course was being taught only to be told by the tutor that there were vacancies and he would be glad to let us start immediately. We were incensed with anger as we went back to the reception desk in the main lobby. I confronted this woman with condemnation of her lies and her determination not to enrol us. The commotion got the attention of an apparently senior person who apologised and enrolled us there and then.
We were almost deceived into giving up, not only our future but the future of our families and of our country.

Racism was so evident and widespread that even a simple clerk working at a reception desk could take it upon herself to institute this kind of behaviour and yet have no qualms about how she negatively affected other people's lives. I asked myself.

- What in God's name possessed her to do such a wicked thing?
- Was it because she thought that we were not worth ten minutes of her time even though enrolment of new students was part of her duties?
- Did she deliberately use her position of trust to discriminate against two black men whom she had never met?
- Was she so incensed with hatred and bigotry to deny us our basic human rights?

This was not my first encounter with Racism of this nature and I was deemed to experience many more.

She was probably saying to herself:-
'Smile with them, tell them a pack of lies, make it look genuine and they will go away accepting what was said, after all, I am white. They must believe me'.

We are still being treated in a subservient manner by people who still believed that they are superior because of their white skin rather than their intellect.

After resigning from my job in Crawley, I applied for a job with a company making radar equipment. My presence was not appreciated there by some of the top machine operators because I was outperforming them and as a result received higher wages because of the bonus system that was operated by the company.

I subsequently moved to a company making marine equipment. I desperately wanted to achieve my goal and as a result of my ambitions, moved around from one company to another in an effort to gain as much knowledge and experience as possible in as short a time span as possible.

I was always treated with a degree of apprehension partly because of my positive approach and therefore the manager of the marine engineering establishment was very cautious and sceptical when he offered me the job. During the interview, I gave a comprehensive list of my skills and experience to date. Although I answered all the knowledge questions correctly I got the impression that he did not believe that I could do the work but he gave me the job anyway. He seemed desperate for someone to start straight away in order to clear the backlog of orders.

This assumption was made because of a sarcastic comment made (*now is the moment of truth*) when he gave me a job to complete which was shunned by the other engineers in the factory. I successfully completed the job. I don't know if he was overjoyed at how well the job was done or disappointed that he did not have an excuse to dismiss or belittle me.
I beggar the question. Why did he hire me if he had doubts about my ability?

I soon moved on after a few months still sticking to my quest to condense as much knowledge as possible in a shortened time span. This led me to a company where I was engaged in the manufacture of Gyro Compass parts. I was still attending evening classes 3 hours per evening 3 evenings a week. The supervisor became aware of this and had the audacity to tell me that I was wasting my time which he thought could have been better spent working longer overtime hours for a higher wage packet.
'Money is not every thing' and the sacrifices made, paid off later.

I was getting on in years and realised that I had to make the best use of my youth and my education while I had the opportunity. I was afraid of reaching an age which would make it difficult for me to be given the opportunity to excel.

I persevered for 2 years before re-applying to the 'Government Training Centre' (MSC) to do an Engineering Design course which lasted one year. I thought that my previous experience as a Building Draughtsman in Barbados and the fact that I was making good progress in my other engineering studies would benefit me. I had no problems in completing this 12 month intensive course successfully with the aid of a Government grant and by doing odd jobs to supplement this grant so as to support my family.

I continued to work in the industry and pursued my educational qualifications. By then I had a total of 5 years engineering experience under my belt and answered an advertisement for a vacant post as an instructor at my previous Training Centre. The idea of going back as an instructor to work along side my former teacher and role model appealed to me. He was also excited at the prospect of this as I was a product of his tutelage and he wanted his colleagues to know about it.

After my application was accepted, I went through 3 stages of rigorous interviewing which included written, oral and practical tests. The first interview sought to test my knowledge base and was carried out by a panel of 4 senior engineering instructors.

On entering the room, I realised that I was not the only one who felt nervous and intimidated. There I was, a black man confronting this panel of white experienced engineering personnel who were ready to pounce.
I approached and greeted each one with a firm handshake. There was nervous tension in the room. I made a joking comment and the atmosphere quickly changed. My technique was to engage them in dialogue and keep them as busy as I could for as long as possible. The idea was to give them less time to bombard me with questions. The strategy worked and I left the room feeling confident.

I often wondered if I was the first black applicant this panel had faced and that was why they were a little wary of how to approach me for fear of infringing the relatively new 'Race Relations Act'.

The next stage of the interview was the written knowledge test. My experience of the past 5 years and my college education was very helpful and I sailed through with out any problems. The practical test was a bit more difficult with a time limit imposed. Unfortunately I did not meet the time limit imposed and failed that part of the interviewing process.
I engaged the help of my former instructor who advised me to ask for a re-test of the practical since my other results were exceptional. The request was granted and this time I was better prepared. The examiner was quite flexible and I was successful second time round.

I was subsequently appointed to the post and waited patiently for my appointment to be ratified so that I could start achieving what I considered to be my true vocation. There was only one other Black engineering instructor in the country working within the M.S.C. and I was pleased to be the second. I was later informed that the pass rate for instructors was a mere 1.97%. I felt elated and was proud to be among such an elite group.

Naturally, I had to undergo training before being released on a group of unsuspecting engineering trainees. The instructor training college was too far away to make daily journeys and it was therefore necessary to take board at the Instructor Training College.

I recall an incident while taking an evening stroll through the town where I was staying during my training. As I walked along the lonely street I encountered 4 white youths with no one else in sight. I was being taunted by one of them, possibly the 'show off' of the group. As I approached, I crossed the road to where they were standing. The element of surprise caught them off guard. My approach shocked them. The five of us ended up having a friendly conversation. They were just four youths who probably thought that they might have a bit of fun, probably 'chasing me around the town' if I had shown fear and decided to run away from them.
I knew within myself that if there was a confrontation I would not have stood a chance and the best way out of that predicament was to offer friendship.

Communication is often the key to acquiring a peaceful and amicable solution.

The Transition.

I started my new job under the watchful eyes of my former instructor who had been promoted to Chief Instructor during my absence from the establishment. It felt strange to be working alongside other instructors who had helped to train me in the past. Everyone was willing to help me overcome any pitfalls which might have occurred. My knowledge base was good and thankfully everything went smoothly. However I had planned to handle any awkward situations in my own way without the help of anyone else. I was determined to show professionalism. It would not have done my career development any good if I had to call for help at the first sign of trouble.

I recall an occasion when returning from Leave to find that one new white trainee had joined my class during my absence. As usual I was at my desk before the trainees arrived and was approached by this new trainee with a look of bewilderment and suspicion in his eyes. I, in turn became very anxious as to what was in store for me. As it happened, he turned out to be one of the best students of that group, not only in his progress but also in the manner and respect he displayed throughout the duration of his training. He brought his partner in to meet me on the last day of his course. I later asked him at the end of his training, what were his first thoughts on seeing a black instructor. He replied "you don't want to know".

My trainees were predominately white and in some cases older than I was. I treated them with respect and got the same in return. I was determined not to tolerate any nonsense from my trainees, my colleagues nor my superiors. My past experience with bigots caused me to harden my approach and be ready to deal with anyone with racist tendencies. I soon found that this was not necessary because of the type of trainees and colleagues that I had encountered. I believed that I was respected mainly for my knowledge and my ability to pass it on effectively. Gratitude was shown by each individual student at the end of the course. I was inundated with bottles of wines, spirits and other gifts by grateful students. They often brought members of their family to meet me who in turn showed appreciation for what I had done to help them achieve.
Job satisfaction greatly outweighed my salary.

Teaching was my forte.

My success as a Government Training Centre Instructor led my superiors to feature me on Television commercials and also in National Newspapers advertisements in an effort to attract more black applicants for instructor posts and also for the initial production engineering training. At last the 'doors' seem to be opening at an alarming rate and more black people were taking advantage of the opportunities offered.

"I didn't realise that Black men got these jobs".

This was a comment made to me by another Black man on one of the many 'open days' staged at the Training Centre by the Manpower Services Commission (M.S.C). The advertisements seemed to have made some impact. I felt proud that I had played an effective part in this changing process.

CHAPTER 10

Hypocrisy and all.

My newly found 'celebrity' status made me a big hit with my hypocritical white neighbours. We were an isolated black family at that time. I was now the 'toast of the town', 'the famous black neighbour'. I was constantly being invited to house parties and was now active in advising and helping the neighbours in matters which demanded some academic ability. Whereas before, my family and I were hardly ever spoken to. I found myself helping the youngsters on the estate with their homework problems and offering them advice on their career development issues. The change in attitudes was astounding.

My son was the only black boy on the estate and the only one in a school of around 500 boys. Life for him on the estate was O.K. with his contemporaries who were not indoctrinated by the bigoted adults. He was a talented footballer and I realised that this could be a disadvantage for him in relation to his academic studies. My son was given the opinion that he could make it as a professional footballer and this tended to divert his attention from his studies. In those days that was only a dream for a young black boy. In reality it was almost impossible. That is why I insisted that more attention was paid to his studies as he would need a back-up plan.
He never made it as a professional footballer.
He was constantly being bombarded with racist taunts from other boys at the school, getting the blame for things he didn't do and also being punished for reacting when being constantly pushed.

I regularly visited the school to protest at the number of times he was taken from his lessons in order to play football and also to discuss his academic progress. This practise would not normally have bothered me if the school had made provisions for him to catch up on what he had missed. The constant battle with the school and myself carried on with promise after promise until something was done to compensate.

Being one of the very few black boy in the area seemed to have attracted the attention of some of the less friendlier police officers and my son was stopped and searched without probable cause on occasions. He was once walking with a group of his school friends. He was the only black boy in the group and was singled out by an officer in a passing police car who proceeded to goad him by asking him questions such as 'where is the knife you were carrying' and then suggesting that he was throwing stones at the police car. This harassment was temporarily stopped after his mother and I made an official complaint on our son's behalf. We were later visited by a police complaints officer who apologised and assured us that it won't happen again. We moved to a different area but to no avail.

However, my son always resisted the provocation of these over zealous police officers and kept himself safely within the bounds of the law.

My son eventually finished school without having achieved his maximum potential. He continued his education at college where he was moderately successful in his quest to become an electronics engineer. My three girls attended a Grammar school and were more successful in their chosen areas but there was still some contention between the school and myself over the choice of examinations for my youngest daughter.

About the time that she was due to take her exams, the government had introduced a lesser recognised examination; Certificate of Secondary Education. (CSE) for students who were thought to be not capable of passing the more difficult 'General Certificate of Education' (GCE) in any particular subject. My daughter was put in this category for a subject in which I thought she was quite proficient. This prompted protest from myself and I was subsequently informed by the 'head of year' that it was better to have a CSE rather than nothing. At that time the CSE was not recognised by employers or Further Education colleges as an adequate qualification and was therefore not worth having. I was proved to be right about my daughter's ability when the exam results were returned. My daughter was awarded the highest possible pass for that subject which was deemed to be the equivalent of the GCE grade 'C'. The Certificate of Secondary Education (CSE) was later withdrawn by the Ministry of Education amidst some controversy and the more recognised GCSE (*General Certificate of Secondary Education*) was adopted.

Pearson Nurse

It was interesting to note that all of my efforts and confrontations with my children's teachers were generally ignored until it became known to them that I was also an educator.

CHAPTER 11

Lessons learnt from teaching in a college environment.

I transferred as a relief instructor to a Government Training Centre nearer to my home. This was extremely good for me as I saw the opportunity to booster my knowledge as well as learning new skills in other branches of engineering. My duties included substituting for instructors of any discipline who were either sick or on holiday. During the time spent in my new post, I decided that I needed to progress further and thus enrolled on a Teaching Certificate course which would qualify me to Lecture at a Technical College. This was successfully achieved but not without having to argue my case with one particular lecturer who would congratulate me for presenting a first class lesson and would then mark me down for exceeding the allocated time by a couple of minutes.

After approx 3 years as an Engineering Instructor, I thought that it was time to move on. I applied for a vacant post as a College Lecturer in Mechanical Engineering and was successful in getting the job. Up to this time I was successful with every application made as an engineer with the exception of one with a large manufacturing company in West London.

On seeing the advertisement, I telephoned. After a series of questions I was told to come in for a formal interview as I seemed to be the right person for the job. I arrived at the agreed time and was taken to the manager with whom I had previously spoken. I soon realised that this was a hopeless venture and a wasted journey. On seeing me and without bothering to interview me for the advertised position, he immediately offered me a job as a labourer which entailed loading metal bars into machines and keeping around the machines tidy. I turned away without responding and left the building in disgust. I did not fill in an application form and thus stated my ethnicity and my West Indian accent was not detected on the telephone.

Therefore I could only conclude that he had not expected to see a black man and proceeded to humour me with the downgraded position.

The interview for the lecturer's post went smoothly. The interview panel consisted of a total of seven people. Four at my first interview was bad enough but seven? I employed the same tactics as previously used for the instructor's job. I talked around the answer and joked at every opportunity I got. It was a relaxed atmosphere and it paid dividends.

"You answered the questions in true Lecturer's style".
That was the reply I got from the Principal after the interview. I knew that the job was mine even before the panel had deliberated. I was confident that the interview had gone in my favour.

There were two black lecturers in the department along with a number of white male lecturers and technicians. I was given a warm welcome by my new colleagues who immediately rallied around to give me all the help and support that was needed to survive in this new environment. I immediately felt relaxed and became closely attached to one of the black lecturers and one of the white lecturers. The white lecturer later became my boss as well as my friend and confidant. These two people were instrumental in my baptism to further education. My first impression of the second black lecturer was not good. My suspicions were soon to be realised when I was the subject of one of his negative reports to my senior lecturer. This negativity was bourn through ignorance and also the neglect on his part to upgrade himself with the current technology of the day.

Because my previous job involved training adults to work with specialised machinery in the industry, I was well versed with more up-to-date techniques. I soon realised that by teaching students I had to focus more on the theoretical side, while in training adults I had to concentrate more on the practical aspects of engineering.

I was demonstrating a new technique used to increase the speed of production to a student. It was witnessed by my black colleague who promptly reported that I could damage this newly acquired machine with my 'careless' actions and asked the senior lecturer to warn me. He was made to look like rather stupid and uninformed because the senior lecturer to whom he had reported the incident then asked to be instructed in this new technique. I approached my black colleague to let him know that I found it deplorable that this kind of behaviour would have been practiced by a man of his standing. It so happened that he was the first black engineering lecturer to be appointed to the college and may have selfishly thought that I was a threat to him.

I was soon to realise that teaching 16 to 19 year olds in a college was somewhat different to teaching adults at a Training Centre. Some of these younger students would find ways of missing lessons or be excused from them halfway through. One student used his girlfriend to impersonate his mother and pretended that his grandmother had died in India while she was still alive and in good health living here in England. The grandmother excuses were generally used by most of these class cheats when they wanted to abscond.

I found that the adults were more receptive to their education and followed instructions to the letter. I always had 100% attention with these well disciplined students. In contrast, some of young apprenticed students were not always interested in what they were doing and this sometimes presented a challenge to my ability to keep them excited at the prospect of gaining meaningful qualifications which would have secured their future and give them a better salary with better prospects of advancement. Earning a higher wage always appealed to them. Some employers even offered financial incentives to their apprentices for passing exams.

Some misguided students believed that because they were working alongside a skilled person and possibly doing the same job, (*under supervision*) that they were entitled to the same wage as the senior person with whom they were working. Some were diverted from their studies through the lure of higher wages. These were often the students who either were not well off financially and had to pay dearly for living expenses and therefore could not afford to stay in full time education or those who had the lack of foresight and often gave up their education and training for menial jobs which paid a slightly higher wage than they were getting as apprentices because of the job titles they were given at the time. These jobs were given titles such as 'manager, supervisor etc. in mainly fast food outlets. In fact, any title which clouded the imagination of the more gullible person to entice them to work long unsociable hours was adopted by these companies who it seemed targeted mainly black young men and women.

During my first year at the college and being the 'new boy' in the eyes of the students, I invariable found that there was always one student who wanted to display his prowess in front of the others. This was demonstrated either by the acquisition of a small amount of information relating to the subject or simply by behaving badly during the lesson. Some of them made it obvious that they did not appreciate me teaching them but they would still approach me for advice and information relating to their studies. This behavioural problem was also associated with a minority of black students who wanted to show off to their white contemporaries. So uninformed were some of our black youngsters that one black lad revealed to one of my black colleagues that he intended joining the 'National Front' because his 'friend' was a member. This young black man needed guidance and true friendship and clearly did not realise what his 'friend' stood for.

(The National front is a racist group opposed to the existence of Black people in England. They spread racist propaganda and call for black people to be repatriated to their countries of origin).

I recall an incident with a class of 4th year students preparing for their final exams. This was a serious group of students who were concentrating deeply on problems posed to them during the lesson. One student thought that he would try to disrupt the lesson by continuously asking questions not related to the lesson. It was obvious what his intensions were and one robustly built student emerged from the back of the class room, approached the disruptive aggressor, held him by his lapels and instantly head-butted him to the applause of the other students. He then turned and said to me, "you can continue now sir". This took me completely by surprise and that was the last time the lesson was disrupted by him or any other student of that group. The students of that era were generally well behaved and focused. It was then that more women started drifting into engineering and I did my best to encourage them by getting an article published to this effect in the local newspaper which yielded some results; not as good as I had anticipated but it was a start.

* * *

The college thrived on achieving good results and was rated as one of the best in the country for engineering. My remit was to keep the standards at the highest possible level. I had an excellent group of lecturers and technicians on whom I could rely on for support. I was proud to be a part of this institution and the engineering team was second to none. I decided that this college was most likely to be the place where I would make the most progress and possibly end my teaching career through retirement. I felt relaxed and contented with my new working environment and was determined to make this job as stress free as possible.

I therefore embarked on a plan of approach so as to make my time spent with the students as pleasurable as possible whether or not I was in the classroom with them. I encouraged them to participate in as many activities as possible so as to broaden their knowledge and meet other people from different disciplines in life. I am a keen sportsman and thought that sport was one of the best ways to stimulate one's mind. I also impressed upon them, the importance team sport as a prelude to working as a team member throughout they employment years.

Cricket, table tennis and photography proved to be popular and I spent many extra hours with them in these areas. I used photography as a hobby as well as a tool to help them prepare for the presentation of practical projects. I decided to put as much fun into learning as I possibly could.

(*A strategy which proved to be successful over the years*)

As a student, I always found my teachers to be too serious. This had the effect of generating stress in the classroom and resulted in boring and uninteresting lessons. I was determined that I was not going to adopt this counter productive method of teaching. I therefore set about doing anything and everything to keep the students amused and alert throughout the duration of the lessons which generally lasted for up to two hours. The students got used to my methods and antics and often joined in to make the lesson as interesting as possible. It was a huge success and no one fell asleep.

I was now fully established and went about my job with confidence and enthusiasm. I must confess that the long Summer holidays was one of the main attractions of the job. I made my first visit to New York during one of the long the summer breaks to visit my family and decided to compare and assess the possibilities of residence and employment while I was there.

I was somewhat disappointed at what I observed as a visitor to a city renowned for its diversity.

Segregation was common. There was very little integration between the races and the whites occupied the more up-market areas of the city. The streets were always kept clean and well maintained in the white's areas. The situation was somewhat different in the black areas.

I was based in the predominantly black area of Brooklyn and the differences between the black and white areas of the district were immediately noticeable. Rubbish on the streets, potholes in the roads, rundown buildings etc. in the black communities were common sites. It seemed as though these areas were neglected by the authorities. Whether there was a shortage of funds or manpower; and based on the negative comments from individuals of the black community, one can only assume.

During my stay, I attended an open air concert on the grounds of a local school where some of the popular West Indians entertainers were brought in by the City Authorities to perform for the people in the black community. The concert was a great success but in my opinion, the finale was somewhat tainted when an official from City Hall appeared on the stage to induce a vote of thanks to himself for paying the performers from the city's budget in order to give the black people of Brooklyn a free concert. This appeared to be a political 'con' in order to divert the community's attention from the real issues as noted. ie ; rejuvenation of the district in which the black people resided. There was an indication in his speech that the black community of Brooklyn should be 'thankful for the small mercies' afforded to them.

I was pleased to leave New York and return to an English environment where race relations were better.

CHAPTER 12

Bigotry from the top; 'Chance in a million'

Sometime later, there was a vacancy at a neighbouring college which I thought would be better for me as far as travelling was concern. After paying a fact finding visit to the college I realised that it would be better not to apply for the post because of the frigid atmosphere which existed in the staff room. It was then that I realised the working environment in which I currently worked, was the best that I had encountered through out my working life in England. It would have been silly to resign my post there. I continued for approximately 26 years until I retired at the age of 63; not because I had enough of teaching but because of the politics that had now engulfed education and turned a once enjoyable occupation into a depressing chore.

The newly appointed principal did not help matters and was an instant let down in the eyes of many of the lecturers. The departmental lecturers were once summoned to a room for a meeting with the principal. I was first to arrive and found him waiting. I extended my greetings as one would and his response was mute. I did not pay much attention until my white colleague entered soon after with the same greeting. The principal's response was immediate and friendly as with every other white staff member entering the room. Naturally, I wondered why. I was later informed that this principal was seen on a security camera on another campus removing posters which invited black staff members to a meeting organised for black staff.

It is interesting to note that the 'Black Staff Members' group was encouraged by this same person. The Black staff meetings, when convened, merely acted as a forum for disgruntled black staff to unload their ill feelings about the unpleasant things going on around them. The group was given no power and therefore was unable to redress any occurring situations. Was this another insincere act by this principal to remove suspicion of racist bigotry?

* * *

My promotion

It was not all plain sailing. There were very few awkward moments but the overall experience was one that I will cherish. After having established myself and with a few years experience into the job, an internal vacancy was advertised. I never applied for the post because of an experience I had with one of the senior management team soon after I started the lecturing at the college.

I was enthusiastic and wanted to bring the college up to date with some of the latest technology of that time. (CNC – *Computer Numerical Control*). Having collected the necessary information, I presented this to the head of department who politely thanked me and informed me that the college could not afford to buy the necessary equipment. I felt disappointed but accepted the excuse given to me at the time. This was unusual for me since I am a very sceptical person but I had no alternative but to take his word.

One week later, I learned that the information I had gathered had been given to one of my white colleagues with a view of further investigation into the possibility of acquiring the equipment and including it into the syllabus. I was excluded from this exercise and this naturally dampened my enthusiasm and discouraged me from forwarding an application for the vacant post since the same head of department was involved in the selection process of the successful candidate. I had foolishly given into the establishment and by doing so fulfilled the beliefs of some of the people who thought that we as black people have limited abilities and very little ambition to move forward.

The vacancy was not filled from the first batch of applicants and to my surprise, the principal approached me and suggested that I apply for the now re-advertised position (*I must point out that this was not the same principal as mentioned earlier*). I attended a formal interview and was given the job which seemed to have been earmarked for me. This was my first promotion and a big boost for me. My salary was increased as well as my responsibilities. Much of my faith was restored.

* * *

The position was for a fractional post of 'Outreach worker' whose main task was to go into the community which was predominately black and basically make the people aware of the programmes which were being offered by the College and also to introduce new courses into the curriculum which would benefit the people in the community and the catchment areas. I thought that this would give me the perfect opportunity to interact with more of the black people in the area and offer whatever help and advice I could. It would also give them an incentive and a sense of pride to see that black people can excel and make changes to their lives and their community. There were many black people with low self esteem and not enough was being done to get them out of the doldrums. There was a youth centre but there was a void in the provisions for the 'twenty fives and over' age groups.

Education was the key factor in all of this and I saw it as my job to encourage more black people to take the initiative and embrace this human practice of teaching and learning which seeks to sustain and enhance one's capacity to discover the significance of life and to develop as a person both in the community and in society as a whole and seize the opportunities which existed in order to give them the capacity to acquire the knowledge of knowing one's attitudes, values and skills which are an integral part of our development and also to answer questions and know the difference between right and wrong. By this time, I was elected to serve as a committee member of the Institute of Production Engineers. (I.Prod.Eng)

One of the unsuccessful white lecturers made a most bizarre comment stating that I was not 'Black enough' to suitably do the job, although interaction with a majority of black people was a necessary criteria to get the desired results. This gave me the impression that he thought that the majority of black people would be more inclined to listen to him because he was white. He seemed to be looking back at the times when intellectual development was denied under the system of slavery and whites dominated the minds of blacks and talked down to them rather than to them. Unfortunately some of the less enlightened whites still think that we are slaves and evaluate us on the basis of skin colour and unfortunately, some of the older generation of black people still act in a subservient manner and racism continues to leave black people to be un-employed with a lack of access to opportunities, earning less money, in lower status jobs, living in the worst housing and more liable to physical attacks.

I soon got into the job and was scheduled a few hours a week for my extra activities. My class contact hours within the college were subsequently reduced in order that I may have time to manage these new responsibilities.

* * *

I started a series of 'DROP IN' classes teaching basic Mathematics and English with the help of another black colleague. The teaching environment had to be less intimidating than that of the college building if we were to attract people of a mature age as well as the younger school leaver who may have had a bad experience while at school. It was especially important to get these young black students back into full time education. I saw this as a way forward and went about the task with earnest. My research was aided by black youth group leaders and door to door canvassing of the predominately black areas of the community. I noted some of the ideas put forward and was ready to put my plan into action.

I approached the local Job centre which was strategically located on the High street and was offered the use of a room already equipped with training facilities. This was repeated at the local Community Centre not far away. A total of four hours per week was dedicated to this cause.

The drop-in facility was widely advertised with the help of volunteers from the local youth centre as well as posters displayed on the premises of the Job centre and the Community Centre. The classes soon became very popular. I encountered many people, both black and white, who had very little knowledge of either subject and they seized the opportunity to educate themselves further. Many of their problems were related to 'everyday' situations such as basic arithmetic, aptitude test for job applications, form filling etc. I came into contact with a local pastor whose main aim was to be able to check the collection money from his church and record it correctly. As a result of my research, some courses were developed and taught at the College in order to fill the voids and meet the wishes and needs of some members of the community.

However, this initiative was to be abolished after approximately 2 years when a new principal was appointed and thought that there was nothing more to be gained from this venture and my talents could well be used elsewhere for future developments.

I was well established in my position and had benefited from the various courses I studied in order to qualify me to do a more effective job. These included such courses as – Student Counselling, Education management, Equal Opportunities and other courses of study designed to give me a better understanding of the different type of students that I was to encounter.

However this valuable knowledge was not to be wasted. I was soon approached again and was asked to take on the role of Senior Pastoral Tutor for the Engineering Department. I accepted this position and soon went about my newly found task in earnest. I was accepted as a father figure by the students who relied heavily on me for guidance and information relating to both their personal lives as well as their future careers and current studies.

I was a disciplinarian and the students respected my 'no nonsense approach' and fairness. My aim was to be as friendly as possible but never to let the students become too familiar with me or I personally with them. By being formal, the student was deservedly given that measure of respect and it was reciprocated. It worked wonders throughout the period of their education at the college and this formality was maintained throughout their undergraduate and post graduate years.

My success as Senior Tutor in the Engineering department was noted and my responsibilities were widened to encompass the Computing and Motor Vehicle departments. Because of the increased workload, I was given newly appointed staff members to help with the tutoring and administrative duties. My working hours were now equally divided between my pastoral duties and my lecturing. I was eventually asked to consider doing the job as Senior Pastoral Tutor on a full time basis. I decided that, as a Lecturer I could do a lot more for the students and still unofficially continue to give them the help and guidance they needed. I declined the full time position as Senior Pastoral Tutor and decided that lecturing on a full time basis was the better option.

CHAPTER 13

The need for mentoring in a secondary schools for black youths; Collaboration of the able: A visit from H.R.H. Prince of Wales.

The Margaret Thatcher years as the British Prime Minister saw a steady decline in the manufacturing industry and many of the larger and more established companies were either downsizing, closing or moving to other parts of Europe and Asia where there was still a demand for manufactured products and above all, labour was cheaper. This resulted in a steady fall of engineering apprentices which meant a reduction of mechanical engineering students and staff. This led to a steady change in the curriculum which was designed by the Government agencies together with leading examining bodies to cater for the emphasis which was now placed on the **Service industry**.

There was also a steady decline in the numbers and the quality of students entering the college to pursue engineering studies. However, many of the 16 to 19 year olds who opted to do the available courses were below the standard required for entry. Much of this was due to the fact that there was an influx of students from non-English speaking countries who had a poor command of the English language. However the college adopted a positive approach to this problem and included extra study in English within the course syllabus for foreign students. Some of the home students also accounted for the poor quality of intake as a result of poor examination results from secondary schooling.

Engineering was now looked upon as a second choice and schools tended to encourage their better students to stay on at school to do 'A' level subjects rather than seek a vocational career at a College of Further Education. The 'not so successful' students who were predominately black were referred to Further Education Colleges. An additional year was added to the course for most of these students in order to bring them up to the GCSE level which is required for entry into a National Diploma course and subsequently University.

Because of the poor standard of education of some of the mainly black Students, I joined a mentoring team catering for black students which had recently started at the local high school.
There was a desperate need as these young black students seemed to have little recourse. There was a cry for help from these students as well as their parents.

The following are extracts from a book of poems composed by the students of the Black Mentoring Group, age 11 to 12 :
And I quote..........

Quiet Thoughts

The truth often hurts
It's plain to see,
Why people would prefer
To have you than me.

I find it so sad,
That people will look,
And judge from the cover
Without reading the book.

You come first
And we get the rest,
We're second-rated
And you're thought to be the best.

Black and white
Can be friends
But to-day it seems
That's where it ends

Pearson Nurse

Asian or Chinese
, Black or White,
Both are pretty
Both are bright.

So if you look closely
You will certainly see,
There is not much difference
Between you and me.

Colours of the rainbow

It's crucial to know racism must go
We don't need a scene, it's evil and mean
Why can't we live a normal life
Without any strife, without any strife.

So let's have a giggle and let's have a hug
Don't be racist, don't be a mug.
Colour is important to each one of us,
A rainbow is a rainbow without any fuss.

The programme was formed under the auspices of the Prince's Trust and was very popular among the black students who were actually queuing up to join the programme. It was very successful with a notable change in the attitudes and development of the 'troublesome' black students who were referred for mentoring.

The attitudes of some of the teachers sent signals of low expectations of their abilities. They were expected to be low achievers and trouble makers. Many teachers encourage black children to devote more time, energy and effort towards athletics and sport as an alternative to academic pursuit. As a black man and an educator I felt that black children needed strong positive black men as role models because children imitate what they see. I therefore encouraged some of my more mature black students from the College where I lectured to become involved as mentors in order to satisfy the demand at the school. They duly obliged.

The success of the program soon reached the ears of HRH. Prince Charles (*Prince of Wales*) who thought it necessary to grace us with his presence at the school in order to take a personal look at what we were doing. Our meeting with the Prince of Wales was highlighted in the College News Bulleting and this resulted in more volunteers from the teaching staff of the College willing to join the programme. The visit naturally attracted the attention of the media and as a result, mentoring became popular among many of the schools in London. Many of those students successfully continued their education after leaving secondary school.

H.R.H. The Prince of Wales visiting students and mentors

Black undergraduates were also being disadvantaged. Again the Prince of Wales came to the rescue. The 'Windsor Fellowship' was started in 1986 and this guaranteed sponsorship for Black and Asian students who satisfied the entry requirements for this opportunity in a lifetime to be given the chance to work at management level with successful companies during their undergraduate years. The noted omission of white student from this program gave the Black and Asian student's equal chances of competing against each other for these much sought after opportunities.

Successful applicants were placed with participating companies as well as with selected Government departments and were guaranteed employment and further management training during their holiday breaks from University. There was also an opportunity for these students to be employed with their prospective sponsors after graduating. I was happy to organise and manage this project at my College for approximately the last twelve years of my teaching career.

Because of this project I was privileged to meet people such as the Rt. Hon. John Major (Prime Minister) as well as one of the most interesting men I've ever encountered: Lord David Pitt : an eminent West Indian and an avid cricket fan. We spoke at length about the things dear to our hearts. Cricket was the main topic.
The education and advancement of black youngsters in this country was also paramount in our conversation.

This subject was of great concern to Lord Pitt. He had become disillusioned with how our young Black children were reacting to the system of education in this country and we debated this at length. Many academically able black men and women had already come to the rescue with the opening of 'Saturday schools' which were inaugurated in order to give our children that extra boost they so desperately needed because of the undermining of black children's self-confidence and the development of negative self-image which intensify a great deal throughout the period of their education. History tells them that their ancestors had been primitive savages who had no prior history to the arrival on the African scene of the white man.

How can we build on what we have so far achieved?

Intelligent communication is often the solution to many situations weather it be personal, political, religious, racial or otherwise. Trust and understanding are the main components. Egotism and selfishness must be eliminated and a wider picture of the concerns of all parties must be taken into consideration. It is imperative that no one should feel left out if we are to successfully integrate into this society.

TOGETHER WE CAN CREATE A SOCIETY WHERE COMMON DECENCY CAN PREVAIL.

After many years concentrating on raising my family and nurturing my career, I decided to re-engage in my cricketing activities. My first game was for the college team where I taught. I was surprisingly asked to open the innings against an established local team and managed a score of 56 runs. After that performance I decided to join my local West Indian cricket team as my children were of an age where they were no longer completely dependent on myself or their mother. My weekends during the summer months were now relatively free to pursue my greatest sporting interest.

Cricket was not only a recreational hobby for the team. To us it was much more. It was a means of interacting socially with other teams (black or white), their friends and families. Cricket helped to maintain our standing as gentlemen and also as exponents of this great game. Interaction with other teams not only involved the team members, but also the wives, partners, children and supporters who filled the coaches when making journeys to play at venues near the seaside or in the remote country areas away from our home ground. The team started as a predominantly black West Indian team but as we progress through the years, we attracted a number of white players to the team. Visits were always reciprocated with the same amount of gusto and enthusiasm from the visiting teams; whether English or West Indian.

The British weather was not always favourable but we were always prepared for disappointments with the weather and had alternative means of entertainment such as calypso music, dominoes, and card games and of course, the occasional pint in the local pub or pavilion with our opponents. There was never a dull moment and the aroma of fried chicken was always present. Everyone had a joke to tell or we would revisit past games and mindfully correct our mistakes or reminisce in our past glory. Supporters were always at the forefront giving advice. The women took great interest and often participated in this extra activity.

The games were always played competitively and in good spirit. There were purely friendly games. No undue pressure was applied in these Sunday games and therefore the atmosphere was relaxed and enjoyable. West Indian cricketers, regardless of the level at which they competed, played a crucial part in helping to integrate into the English society. In the eyes of the English people, all West Indians played cricket even though in reality, some never touched a cricket bat or ball. Some of those who had no prior interest in the game saw it as a means of 'getting accepted' and therefore learnt about the intricacies of the game so that they could be involved in relevant discussions pertaining to the game. It was noticeable that the women were always prevalent in the minds of cricketers with such fielding positions as slips. Long leg, Short leg, square leg......

It was during these cricketing activities that I was privileged in making the acquaintance of some of the more famous West Indian Cricketers such as the likes of:- Sir Garfield Sobers, Charlie Griffiths, Dr. Bertie Clark, Malcolm Marshall, Gordon Greenage, Courtenay Walsh and John Holder.
Malcolm Marshall along with Gordon Greengage and John Holder (*Hampshire player and Test Umpire*) occasionally graced us with their presence during indoor practice when visiting the 'Mickey Stewart' indoor facilities during the winter months.

Having played table tennis since I was a young boy in Barbados, I decided to renew my interest in this sport since it was also a ball game and it served to sharpen my reflexes for the more formidable game of cricket. I played two or three times a week through out the year to keep myself in shape. My skills in this game improved tremendously and I was privileged to play with Seeded players of the English League

CHAPTER 14

The fight for equality and recognition goes on.

It seemed that as black people we were always fighting a battle to be accepted as equals and at the same time paying more for the right to be in the society in which we live, despite the fact that we abide by the law of the land and behave as good citizens should.

Our contribution to the British economy matched that of our white colleagues.

Black workers are taxed at the same levels as their white colleagues.

Since employers and the white society treated black workers as second class, then our contribution should be less.

It is unfair that black people should have to pay equal contributions and then be treated as not being equal.

There was always that 'diehard' element that was not willing to come to terms with the emergence of the diverse society that was fast evolving before their very eyes. It is my belief that some black people still display that slave mentality and look upon the white people as their superiors and treat them as such. It is my opinion that if blacks had taken a more positive stance in those early years and not allowed themselves to be downgraded and disrespected, we would have been far more advanced than we are at present. There might not have been any need to legislate on the issue of equality if we had properly asserted ourselves.

Many white people took 'refuge' in other areas of England which were not yet infiltrated by Black people.
'Having a black neighbour was not fashionable'

As soon as a white family moved out, a black family was almost certain to be sold the house because another white family would not want to move into an area where black people were living. One black family moving into the neighbourhood often caused an exodus of white families. There was always that fear that the value of their property would fall, therefore they had to escape before the inevitable (as they saw it) happened. Black people often bought the properties and were then able to be in close proximity with each other and as a result, lived as a community helping and supporting each other.

Black people gathered at each others homes for many reasons. Whether it is for a prayer meeting, to play cards or dominoes or just for friendly chats over a bottle of rum, these meetings were an integral part of the bond which kept West Indians together as a unit. Life, reminiscent to that in the West Indies, gradually returned and we no longer lived in isolation or fear. To walk along the street and be acknowledged by another black stranger was enlightenment to our existence in this country. One would get that 'not alone' feeling.

* * *

During the years of gradual acceptance by the white society, a classism was emerging in the black communities. Some of those who thought that they had 'made it' socially in the white circles, either by job description, affluent white friends or other, termed themselves the 'black elite' or to put it in more definitive terms 'The Black Bourgeoisie'. They were an insecure group of black people who isolated themselves in a world of their own and were rejected by the black 'working and middle-class' and then shunned by their white 'friends'. They now had nothing in common with neither the black society on whom they 'fed' nor the white society who rejected them as equals. This was sad and they eventually found themselves in a quandary with nothing but the selfishness which was ingrained in their minds.

What we want as black people is economic equality but this can not be achieved when more emphasis among black spenders is placed on unnecessary material possessions charged at inflated prices by predominately white designers who jeer us. The designers and retail outlets would price their goods at about four or five times their true value and strangely enough, this practice often attracted uninformed young black buyers who did not know the true value of their money. There was this myth among particularly young black people, that the more money they paid for their apparel, the better quality they got; which was not always the case and this often promoted violence if some innocent bystander should accidently trod on their feet and dirty the trainers they had bought with, perhaps one or two full weeks' wages.

Many items of clothing seemed to be aimed at the blacks youths because of the known reckless manner in which they disposed of their hard earned money and the white designers seemed confident that, no matter how outlandish or expensive their goods are priced, black youths would buy them even though they can not financially afford to do so.

The designers got richer and more blacks live from hand to mouth in abject poverty, not being aware of the enormous financial input they were making to the success of the people who were jeering them.

On realising that there was an enormous amount of money being earned and carelessly spent in white and Asian establishments by an infinite amount of blacks, it was inevitable that some black entrepreneurs would make an effort to attract as many of those black customers as they could and therefore keep the money within the black circle and thus give the black communities some semblance of economic strength. Unfortunately, there was mistrust and the objective could not be achieved. Some black businesses made an effort to 'cash in' by grossly exaggerating their prices and as a result were not successful in their endeavour. A conscious effort was made by the black shoppers to sustain these businesses out of pure solidarity but the greed of some of the proprietors was frowned upon and this was privy to their own failure in many cases.

There were serious issues of Black on Black. Insurance and mortgage scams were high on the agenda as some unscrupulous blacks agents sought to exploit the people whose trust they had cunningly gained. These were mainly elderly West Indians with a limited education who relied solely on the more well informed to advise and act for them in formal proceedings. Naïve young couples were also duped of their savings by this new breed of confidence tricksters who then had to either flee the country or the areas where they lived in fear of their lives after their horrific deeds were discovered. Sorrowful and heart rendering stories were common tales of woe.

Black people love their music and this proved to be one area in which they gained enormous in-roads but were still exploited because of the apparent lack of knowledge in contractual matters and royalties pertaining to their musical talents. Most black musicians had to rely on established white owned recording studios to publish and market their music but they soon learnt the rudiments of the business and as a result, the Motown Corporation was formed to give black musicians access to a recording studio owned and controlled by black people.

Music along with cricket proved to be the two areas in which black people gained the most recognition and respect from the host nation. The colourful Notting Hill 'Street carnival' which combined the various rhythmic beats and flamboyant costumes of the islands of the Caribbean was seen as an ideal advertisement and introduction to our culture and music and was the brainchild of a fellow West Indian in an effort to emulate the celebrations as they are in the Caribbean and also as a response to the race relations in Britain at the time. It was inaugurated to demonstrate the richness and vibrancy of the West Indian culture in an effort to show how people can interact, live in harmony, fellowship and enjoyment with each other. This was a new experience for the English who embraced the idea and sought to institutionalise it. It is now the biggest street carnival in Europe.

This event now attracts thousands of people from al over Europe but unfortunately, the unscrupulous and lawless element of our society, saw the gathering of these thousands of unsuspecting revellers as fair game for their sordid trade. Be it the illegal distribution of drugs, muggings, drunkenness or some other despicable activity.
This rich and cultured event enjoyed by thousands of people, both black and white, from all over Britain and Europe was infiltrated by youths who recklessly blighted a now respected and honoured tradition by their behaviour. Despite the atrocities, attendance was seen to have increased as if to tell the muggers and pickpockets, 'We will not be deterred'.

CHAPTER 15

The never ending saga of acceptance and denial within the society.

The late African American writer, John Hernik Clarke said: "If we are to change tomorrow, we are going to have to look back with some courage, and warm our hands on the revolutionary fires of those who came before us." As a result, BLACK HISTORY MONTH was established in the USA in 1926 and in England in 1987 in order to enrich cultural diversity.
"Despite the significant role that Africa and its Diaspora have played in the world civilization since the beginning of time, Africa's contribution has been omitted or distorted in most history books". (*Ken Livingston, Mayor of London*)

In an ideal world, education establishments now fully recognise and appreciate the black person's contribution to history and humanity. It is my opinion that such achievements should be celebrated and shared with the world at large all the year round. Our black youths have reasons to be proud of the efforts made by our ancestors in the development and shaping of this world which constantly denies us the right to live as equals.

As soon as one barrier is broken down, another one emerges. It does not matter what position a black person holds or what he/she has achieved he/she is invariable rated as second class within the white society. Black people are still looked upon by the uninformed as sons and daughters of slaves and therefore are assumed to have no place in a society dominated by the sons and daughters of the people who once owned them. This is rather unfortunate as it seems to be indoctrinated in some of the less informed who, despite their lesser positions in society or are of a poorer academic and intellectual standard, still think themselves as superior to black people simply because of their white skin.

This notion of inferiority is further fuelled by racially biased reporting by the media who tend to inflame racial tension and violence within a society. Any incident which involves Black and White perpetrators are generally headed by the word 'Black'. For example: 'Black Riots' even when the disturbances may be purposely started by Whites. Also being called 'animals' by the media shows that element of hatred for the black community and gives the impression that all black people are monsters.

One recalls a black member of the conservative party (*Lord Taylor*) who was said to be a friend of the prime minister of the day. He contested a 'safe' conservative seat in a by-election in a constituency which was known to be a predominantly white upper class community, who in the past, always favoured the conservative candidate during an election. The conservative candidate was not elected on that occasion.

Political representation forms the cornerstone of democracy. In reality, white people appeared to have been contriving to prevent black people sharing power except in a ghetto or slum constituency where they were considered electable.

The consensus of opinion as to why this 'unexpected' result occurred was because the candidate put forward by the conservative party to contest the election was a black person attempting to gain in-roads in a predominately 'White Bourgeoisie' society.

One beggars the Questions.

- Was the candidate deliberately set up to fail?
- Did the conservative hierarchy misread the tone of its constituents at the time?
- Was 'Race' one of the mitigating factors which led to the failure of this candidate being elected to parliament?

One will never know. Our minds are historically plagued with injustice and racism and as black people, we can only assume.

As the years rolled on, more black people were being recognised for their talents but there was still that degree of apprehension in the minds of some of our white Colleagues and the employers. Some of the Blacks people who were successful were referred to as 'pawns' and it was assumed that they were elevated to these higher positions in order to make it appear as though the employer was simply conforming to the recently legislated 'Race Relations Act'. Credit was not often given to the black achiever for his/her progression despite the experience and academic qualification gained. There appeared to be a limit to where a black person could rise in various companies and establishments throughout England.

The Race Relations act of 1976 did little in the eyes of black people to help the cause. It was virtually impossible to prove a case of racial discrimination. There were too many loop-holes in the law and racial discrimination remained largely unchallenged in the courts in many areas for many years.

NOT EVERYTHING IS BLACK AND WHITE.

However, the act was subsequently amended in 2000 and then again in 2003 to include discrimination by the police and public authorities after a number of complaints was made against the police for their handling of black youths.
- How long before some people get over the pre-occupation with skin colour?
- How long until some people get over the conviction that white skin makes them superior?
- How long until they start making racist loudmouths legally and morally responsible for their incitement into hatred?

Spontaneity of the criticism and name calling of one race of people by another who conveniently use their acquaintances within that race to hide their true feelings tend to be most dangerous and hypocritical.

How long before people start living out the true meaning of our creeds, both civil and religious that all men and women are created equal and are precious in the sight of god?

- Black people as well as white people must accept each other for who they are.
- Black people as well as white people have unique features which cannot be attained by either race.

View points differ. There will be mutual disagreements.

- We share common experiences based on our race and culture but we are not all the same.
- We must embrace with open arms to find a common solution and not cowardly let a certain group of people or one person incite this abominable behaviour.
- We are equal but individual.
- We are alike but not identical.

Whatever the reason, both blacks and whites must come to terms with their inner selves and accept the fact that we are one people in the sight of god and I believe that the good Lord did not intend for one group of his people to rein supreme over another.

We as black people must first eradicate that feeling of inferiority among ourselves and at the same time, stand tall and assert ourselves within the true meaning of equality.

Black people must come to terms with a world based on science and we must teach our children accordingly.

We must control our economic fate by mastering the principles which are paramount to the successful development of our countries and communities. It has become an Educate or die situation and the education must start with the parents. Without their input and support, teachers cannot successfully build, expand and reinforce young minds in order to transform them into engineers, entrepreneurs, businesspersons or financiers.

CHAPTER 16

Black nation and black people in general are never out of the firing line and remain the targets for exploitation.

It is interesting to note that black nations are generally the ones to be most affected when economic changes are made by the World's richest nations. Despite the fact that some of the black nations survive on 'shoe string' budgets, more pressure is piled on and the rich nations selfishly become richer. How the Black Nations are therefore expected to survive in this world of so-called equality when unfair tariffs are applied at will, which in the process causes the near collapse of their economies? It would appear that Independent West Indian colonies are still paying compensation in the form of foreign exchange earnings for their freedom and independence from the worlds more powerful countries that blatantly abuse their power and then refer to it as politics.

These practices affect the ability of the black nations to provide the services enjoyed by their richer neighbours. Educational opportunities, jobs, access to decent housing, health care and development of the infrastructure are paramount in a developing country but are sometimes ignored and denied because of the greed of others and the economic injustices sometimes jointly administered by internal forces that tend to collaborate with external forces for their own self gratification.

There seems to be a limit imposed on Black Nations to determine how far they can progress. Unfortunately the lure of money to greedy politicians and others generally helps to promote the suffering of the less fortunate nationals despite the fact that the same country may be rich in agriculture, minerals or oil and if managed properly, wealth could be more evenly distributed in order to increase the economic wealth and welfare of the nation as a whole. Greed and selfishness is often the cause of poverty and depravity in many black nations. Racism of black on black also presents a problem where class distinction is practiced and equality tends to be redefined.

* * *

Stop and Search

There was a glimmer of hope in the early 1980's after protests by black people in response to the police unfair action when implementing the 'Stop and Search' law which was enacted by the British government of the day. The police tended to single out black people more than any other race of people to indiscriminately stop and search.

This practise was soon to be limited and black youths were less intimidated by over zealous and racist police officers. The relationship between the police and the black people improved a great deal and it seemed as though there was mutual respect and a growing confidence in the police over the past two/three decades.

However, a recent draft from the home office on police guidance obtained by Liberty, (*an independent campaigning organisation which works to protect civil liberties and promote human rights*) now sets down new rules that would allow race to be a basis for stop and search by the police without suspicion.

The directive is actually telling the police that they can legally discriminate on the grounds of race. They are not considering the bigger picture or the ramifications of the whole system they are helping to perpetuate.

This action would represent a breach of the Labour Government equality act of 2010 which prohibits race discrimination by public bodies.

But the proposed new guidelines also make it clear that ethnicity may not be used as the sole basis for stopping and searching. (*Mail on Line*)

One wonders who will take 'credit' for this contradiction/interpretation of terms. In the earlier part of the draft, it was suggested that the police had the authority to stop and search on the basis of race. The police seem to be the people doing the dirty deeds while their bosses seem to be 'covering their backs' and setting themselves apart from all responsibility of the actions of their police officers.

As I come to the end of this journey I would like to leave a thought for my readers. Taken from;

Romans 12:3

For by the grace given to me I say to everyone among you not to think of yourself more highly than he ought to think, but to think with sober judgment, each according to the measure of faith that God has assigned him.

END